MONSIGNOR WILLIAM BARRY MEMORIAL LIBRARY
BARRY UNIVERSITY

PZ4.S443 B76
Segal, Fred. cn   010101 000
The broken-field runner / by F

0 2210 0086315 1

Y0-CJI-240

PZ
4   162402
.S443
B76

Msgr. Wm. Barry Memorial Library
Barry University
Miami Shores, FL **33161**

SEGAL

BROKEN-FIELD RUNNER

THE
BROKEN-FIELD
RUNNER

THE BROKEN-FIELD RUNNER

by Fred Segal

The New American Library

Copyright © 1967 by Fred Segal
All rights reserved. No part of this book may be reproduced
without the permission of the publishers.

First Printing

Published by The New American Library, Inc.
1301 Avenue of the Americas, New York, New York 10019
Published simultaneously in Canada by
General Publishing Company, Ltd.
Library of Congress Catalog Card Number: 67-16942
Printed in the United States of America

**TO
JACQUELINE**

THE
BROKEN-FIELD
RUNNER

1

AARON FRANKLIN WAS TALL as a doorway.
He entered rapidly, wiping his hands on a paint rag, and bent down from his enormous height to kiss his mother's cheek. He withdrew and raised his long, thin, heron's body in a painful journey upward, unwinding his joints in the ascent until he stood, opened his arms, and yawned majestically.
He rebelted a paisley scarf about the waist of his canary yellow corduroys and approached his father.
"I'm on to something."
Sol raised his face to await his son's kiss. As he began the journey downward, the boy placed his paper-thin fingers on Sol's cashmere jacket for support. His legs, his elbows, his neck began to bend in metronomic sequence; first his large head, followed prudently by each vertebra, until his body resembled a shepherd's crook, at which time he pressed his lips against his father's forehead and said. "That's my pop."
Sol patted his skinny buttocks. "Nice kid."
"Secular art is willful. Psychological. Personal. Vain and, worst of all, unbeautiful."

"Sit down, big shot."

Aaron frowned. "I don't talk down to you. You don't know what secular painting is, and for that matter, you don't know one color from the next."

Sol grinned. The kid had gumption.

"So?"

"Don't call me 'big shot.'"

He tucked the napkin under the collar of his orange shirt. "Formal painting is concerned with the picture's surface. The act of not painting, of waiting for that surface to speak, requires a passivity, a vulnerability modern painters are incapable of."

Sol lit a cigar. "Get Rose," he said, pointing the lit end towards the kitchen door.

His wife Alma rang the silver dining bell. Rose entered carrying a covered silver tray. She moved morosely and put the tray at Aaron's left. She uncovered it and retreated, a pretty girl in a white uniform.

"If I eat with you, you'll have to talk to me," Aaron said. He filled his plate with roast beef, hash brown potatoes, and sliced cucumbers. He gestured at Sol with a fork. "Tomorrow I leave for college. While I'm gone, you'd better consider me and where we go from here, you and I."

"College! I'm offering him a multimillion-dollar deal, and he picks college! Where's the sense? A kid like him, a tall kid. He could be anything."

Aaron lowered his head.

His mother asked him to eat.

"I'm not anything if I'm not a painter. I'm going to college to find out."

"What if you're not? What if Archie Fellows laughs?"

Aaron smiled mysteriously. "He won't laugh. I may be bad, but not laughable."

2

"What would you do if he laughed?"
"I'd smack him."
His mother cautioned him. "You're overtired."
Aaron tasted the meat, and lowered it to his fist and onto the floor where the Airedale, Pal, waited patiently.
"Eat your food. Don't give it to the dog," Alma said.
"You're right. Have her take it away."
Sol said, "You're trying to kill your mother."
"Don't shout at the boy."
Aaron chewed a slice of cucumber. "All right," he said wearily. "I'll eat."
Chewing embarrassed him, as did many things. Each morning, he awakened to a recent embarrassment. He talked too much. His mouth opened in the morning and remained opened until sleep closed it. He talked for another reason: to find out what he was talking about. Being nineteen was difficult: a no-man's-land. At eighteen he hated his father. At nineteen he had outgrown the idea. Optimistic yet wary, conscious of the year behind where hell was, with pimples and unexpected hair.

As his father puffed his big cigar and gazed dreamily at a list of party invitations, the boy listened to the crickets. Dogs barked distantly and powerboats roared on Long Island Sound. These suburban noises once confused him. An adolescent, uneasy with unfamiliar countrysides, he had listened in deep depression. The exposure of sun and grass and open space held nameless terrors. He had mistrusted nature; the sissified crocus, the daffodil. Timid blades of refertilized grass had a proprietary air; none of the seasons heeded him; roses bloomed without his knowledge; pansies simpered behind his back while lilacs grew and smelled themselves. Leaves came and went, from lime-green to grizzled-brown, falling, raked and burned. They pervaded the country with smoke and cheap nostalgia.

He rubbed his long neck and looked at Sol, who six years earlier had decided to move here.

"Breathe the air," he said. "Good for kids."

When he had announced this fact in their Park Avenue duplex, Aaron had every intention of hitting him. Then, of course, they'd been the same size. Now it was too late. He had outgrown his enemy and, Gulliver-like, gazed down on his little father and noted with melancholy the loss of a good opponent.

Sol said, "What a night. Smell the Sound." He stood. He lowered his head and cleared his throat. "I'll take a walk. Breathe the air."

They heard the screen door shut behind him and listened to his steps on the gravel driveway.

Alma said, "I like your shirt."

"It's the brightest I could find. Do you think it's too orange?"

She covered her face momentarily with her napkin. "What do I know about color?"

He agreed. "I'm going to college tomorrow. I don't want to offend anyone."

"Wear it. Wear whatever you want. You won't be young forever."

He examined her as she sipped her coffee. A mother's face is unlike any other, because no other face is seen so often; the opinions, prejudices, and vagaries are all recorded and magnified; each pore, each shadow is too important to forget—a giant screen upon which all hope is cast, all love, contempt, and joy. The face—that automated computer through which his data cards passed, through which his life was judged. Her lashes, her brows, her lips. They mirrored him. His father was a relative. He was of her, she had created him through some alchemy that only mothers know. He had sprung alive at seven pounds from out her magic trick. They were the same, or parts of the same.

Impulsively, he pushed his plate back and excused himself.

"Don't go. Finish your dinner."

"No. I'm leaving for college. I want to hear him."

She sighed. "Don't let him catch you."

"He never has."

"It embarrasses him."

He stood carefully until he had reached his full height.

"Well, don't stay too long. You'll catch cold in that loft."

He left the house and loped along the grass until he reached the garage. He climbed up the outside ladder carefully. He forced his long body through a small window and entered the narrow space above the garage. There, hidden and cramped behind lawn furniture, inner tubes, and warped screening, he heard his father play ragtime and wondered how so angry a man could evoke such beauty from an upright piano.

From his perch, through gaps in the flooring, he watched him, the adversary, the tyrant who hit the old piano, its ivory browned by wet cigars. He made it preen. It recalled past glories as the keyboard perked and rode on triumphantly beneath his short, fat fingers.

Aaron immersed himself in an ocean of ragtime and considered his life. He had outgrown his father. He had discarded him like tight underwear. No man is a hero to his son, he thought. He had seen Sol in a union suit. He had seen him out of breath on the station platform, and, although he had the documents to prove it, it was difficult to imagine him a hero. The photograph of him in his trench coat, looking rakishly out, his leg thrown over a studio sandbag, seemed to belong to another, a more sensitive, thinner man. The medal and the laminated citation in the glass case were apparently authentic. They bore his name. In the first World War, he had been fearless. His courage under fire won him a field commission, a personal recommendation from General Pershing, and the Silver Star.

There he sat, hitting the keyboard, fixing his world with bright blue eyes, giving no quarter, demanding everything, looking as he must have then, when, crazed with lice and frostbite, he advanced alone and knocked out two machine guns. He had murdered six surprised Germans and indignantly seated himself on their sandbags.

Aaron didn't believe in war. Killing was too personal to be trusted to groups.

Down below, "Muhlenburg Joys" boomed like a cannon. Once, on Park Avenue, he had discovered his parents hugging each other like adolescents. He went to his room without a word and seriously oiled his bowie knife. He believed in those days (he was barely fifteen) that sons have no bandage to bind their pain. Like migratory workers, they travel aimlessly from one day to the next. Now, dressed like a dandy, in expensive corduroy and suede and flannel, his hair long, his mouth firm like some town marshal, he felt his approaching manhood and prepared himself for the day he would forgive his father and mother for interfering, for being his keepers instead of his peers.

His father finished and slumped, scratched his nose, whistled noisily, and began again, his hands wildly pounding the keyboard, his feet stamping furiously. And, as if a veil had been removed, his face showed itself clearly. Aaron saw the particular set of the chin, the thrust of the neck. He quickly shut his eyes. Feeling nervous, uneasy and overheated, he glanced furtively downward and averted his eyes.

A cramp in his leg caused him to move. The wood creaked and he held his breath in fear that Sol would discover him; but the music continued. His neck itched, and the cramp persisted, so he carefully backed out so that his toes hung out the window.

He wiggled his body until his waist rested on the sill; then, silently, he gripped the ladder with his suede shoes and climbed to the ground.

With regret, he realized he would spy no longer on the old man. The dreamy expression he had seen was too complicated to be violated. A child might watch and misunderstand. It was sex he saw. Sol revealed himself. The plump body seemed braced for orgasm, not melody, so he vowed never to spend another moment dissecting that solitary face. He walked across the driveway and down a path to the studio his father had built him the year before.

As he entered, he heard the faint sound of Sol's piano.

Paintings faced him from all available space. He regarded them unhappily. They were too loud, too personal. The painting he had finished that day was merely an underpainting, a beginning, a sketch.

Earlier, he had rushed about the canvas with a charcoal stick and soon she appeared, plump and spreading in fleshy folds: a huge hoop of a woman. Whistling and stamping his feet in agitation, he had attacked his tubes of paint and spread out mounds of color on his milk-glass palette. Grabbing at a brush, he had gotten the thing started in a desperate advance, shoving and sliding his brush along the slippery paint, pressing on, never pausing, with no thought of failure. Orange was spread on the lady's back and down her thighs and out her toes. Vermilion eyes stared from her face with cobalt eyeballs expressing nothing. A mouth with bee-stung lips, done in green; naked canvas, as if by accident, formed her teeth. Squinting, he had leaped ahead, dragging paint across her neck to form a violet scarf. His whistling had grown shrill; he pounded the floor. Details appeared beneath his brush: fingernails and bloodied toes. He had stuck his brush in a pile of pink and added arched eyebrows. He had shot his arm forward and painted round persimmon nipples. He had rapidly completed a pubic triangle of Van Dyke brown and, breathing hard, had dropped his brush and slumped to a chair.

2

SOL KNEW THE KID HAD BEEN UP THERE. He heard the wood creak over his head. He heard him enter the loft and he heard him leave it and he thought: the hell with it. He struck the piano keys with all his strength. His short body bent from overweight, shortness of breath, and unexorcised demons, he began again: "It's a long way to Tipperary," and forgot, temporarily, the furies who fell upon him with migraines, ulcers, and tempers.

In bad moments, when he hated his son for spying, bits of spittle flew from the corners of his lips; his plump body swelled with hate; a zeppelin of outrage and vengeance, he stomped the keys.

Things went badly that day. He had checked into a good hotel in the afternoon with a bottle of laxative and had drunk it in one gulp. He had purged himself of evil in that bathroom in midtown New York, and weak with punishment, had collapsed on the bed, his body limp and sinless, in a personal state of grace. Toilets were his confessional, wherein he earned his goodness. The laxative was his only weapon. He attacked evil with enemas.

His wife, he thought, beginning another chorus, served him stoically, adjusting herself to his moods like a faithful radar. She had depersonalized herself in the process. If, at night, from the depths of failure, he tore at her, she turned quickly in the bed for his spasm.

Not always, he thought, giving himself the benefit of doubt. Sometimes he reached for her on a Sunday afternoon, or possibly in the early morning, before dawn, with such a tenderness that a faint stirring of youth and love returned to her servant's body.

Without her he felt incomplete. If she remained in her chair reading while he retired to bed, he feigned such weariness, she would clasp his waist and help him climb. Should she develop a cold, he raged about her bedroom, insisting she medicate herself and keep covered. On those days, instead of commuting to New York City, he sat by her side, memorizing her face, recording her slightest signs of recovery, feeling her pulse, fighting her fever with liquids and aspirin, and growling at the family doctor whose inadequacies in the face of colds disgusted and angered him.

Sol spoke from his vigil in the chair.

"She'll be on her feet in no time. A matter of hours. A day at the most!" He glowered at the doctor and eyed him maliciously. "We'll lick this thing without you."

Alone, he squeezed her hand and kissed her pale cheek.

"Keep covered," he cautioned.

"Go to work, Sol." She withdrew her hand. "For God's sake, go to the office."

He grinned and jabbed his thumb at the door. "That's one hell of a doctor we have. That's some find."

In moments of tenderness, when love suffused his fat body, he remembered music. Once, at the age of fourteen, he had played piano in a Boston burlesque house.

It wasn't until twenty years later, when he'd made his first half million, that he returned to the piano. He had one at his office in New York and one at his home in North Neck. Both uprights, he kept them out of sight whenever possible. They bespoke softness. He went to music surreptitiously.

His son Aaron, a boy of nineteen, and his wife Alma were more precious to him than himself. He spoiled them both and bullied them. He overwhelmed them with energy, ruthlessness, and generosity. He broke their spirit with outrageous tempers and calculated deceits, then drew them back to him with new enchantments, gifts of automobiles, furs, tennis rackets, theater tickets, dinners at Pavillon and the Colony. Laced with vulgar sentimentalities, self-pity, pride, and common vanities, he struck at their souls with his barrage of energy, some of it treacherous, most of it so personal and urgent that he had no words, no literature to save him. Thus, he bought them presents and squeezed them tearfully and ordered them to bed.

Without Alma, he feared for his soul. She was his church. His protector. Without her, once, on a business trip to Athens, when the ship was six days out, he felt such loneliness and utter abandonment, he took the three single ladies who shared his dining room table into his stateroom and drank whiskey with them until four in the morning, when, weak with fatigue, he fell on top of the one (a retired schoolteacher, a woman of fifty, at least) who remained awake and sober enough for roistering. Her two companions, it turned out, were merely feigning sleep and sat bolt upright as Sol prepared to enter. He paid them off. He gave them each a hundred dollars in traveler's checks and pleaded with them to forgive him. He had no right. He missed his wife terribly . . . the whiskey (he seldom drank) . . . He looked at them beseechingly. They took the money. They rummaged drunkenly around, found their purses, and stumbled away, the three elderly ladies.

The next morning he feared facing them at breakfast and considered eating in his cabin. A knock on his door brought him wide-awake. It was the ladies. They had prepared a tray, the center of which contained one rose. The remainder was breakfast: eggs, bacon, juice, and coffee. They placed it on his lap and, giggling, retreated. He read the note.

"You are our rose," it said.

He blushed and ate their food nervously.

On the boat he saw the schoolteacher. She had sat beside him and pushed the lounge chair close enough to rub her bony knee against him. Proud that he had chosen her above the others, she called him her "adventure."

She told him about her husband and their life in Euclid, Oklahoma. And he, the little Jew from Boston, looked at her with wonderment. In her face he saw the covered wagons, the untamed frontier, a foreign America. When she innocently told him of her poverty, of her husband's death (their one mule had kicked him to death after twelve years of servitude), his eyes filled. When she crammed the traveler's check in his pocket, saying she should pay him instead of vice versa, he reached for her arm and led her to his stateroom.

As vulnerable, guileless, and innocent as the air must be in Euclid, Oklahoma, she watched him gratefully as he undid her stays and corsets.

"I'll be your mule," he said, blushing at his sentimentality.

"You mustn't kick Sally," she said sweetly, covering her nakedness with her hands. Then, towering above him, she leaned and kissed his pink face.

She had probably died at seventy. Each Christmas, she sent him a card, unsigned, from Oklahoma. For the past two Christmases, no card had arrived.

He reentered the house and found his wife waiting. She said: "You've got the energy of a young man. My father knew that about you."

He scoffed. "Your father! He never seized America!"

"He loved me."

"That's not enough. You must love America. That man only spoke Yiddish." Finishing his coffee, he belched.

The boy was a disappointment. He had hoped to find a friend, a little pocket of warmth in the house. But, from birth, the kid had watched him warily, as if he feared and hated him. It was a lot to ask, having an enemy under your own roof.

"I have some good news."

She leaned forward.

He tugged at his lower lip and spoke with what seemed to be a touch of regret. "Yes. Freidlander's people finished the statement. It's amazing. The figures are there in black and white."

"Oh, Sol," she said. "I'm very proud of you."

He sighed. "I did it."

"You really did. I'll tell the boy."

He beamed at her. "I'll tell him. We'll see what he thinks of the old guy!"

"I knew it would happen. You can laugh, but Father knew it as well."

"I never liked him. People should be Jews on their own time. My father assimilated."

"Polar bear swimming! He was a health faddist, not a person!"

He agreed. "Maybe he overassimilated. Maybe he was crazy, but he loved America. He knew his history, from 1776 to the Civil War. He knew about Tulsa and Denver and the

13

California Gold Rush." His eyes closed dramatically. "He loved this great country, and he never left Boston."

"You're a better man than he. You're a millionaire. He never earned a nickel."

Sol flushed. "Money is no answer."

The statement his accountants had prepared that morning showed him to be, after taxes, a millionaire.

"That's a lot of money. Finally! We have the party."

Old Sally had loved him. She really had. God, what a trip. Young enough to be her son, he had helped her in and out of chairs and had treated her like a queen. An old lady, really. But, to him, an exotic from a foreign land. After all, Euclid, Oklahoma, doesn't come along every day. Gentiles resembled men, no matter what sex they were, and Sally reminded him of George Washington. He had to laugh at times, because nobody goes to bed with history. He rode her day and night. Fresh from the American prairie, she smelled of wheat and clover and talked like a rube.

He was the first Jew she had ever seen. His hair was blond then, and that, plus his blue eyes, confused her. Once, settling back on his narrow cot, as the boat creaked beneath them, she looked at him with affection. Touching her blue-gray waves, she said, "You Jewish people are darned sweet. I mean it from the bottom of my heart. Nobody ever treated me with swell manners. Not even my husband. He was a good man. But, your Jewish skin is soft as a woman's."

He looked at the list of names. This party represented a promise he had made himself when he had returned from the war, out of money, without prospects, a twenty-two-year-old lieutenant with a Silver Star from a grateful nation and sixty-three dollars in his AEF overcoat.

Having led his company from the arch at Washington Square, up Fifth Avenue, past the women in hobble skirts, politicians in derbies, and cheering children waving flags, he had returned to Boston to find his partners gone, his mother dying, and his sisters as passively dependent as the day he had enlisted. It was like old times, they said happily, touching his medals and relating the gossip of two years.

He deserved the party now. One million dollars, tax free. He was the fulfillment of the American dream.

He imagined the boy's face when he told him. So doing, his spirit sagged.

"Why is he leaving?" he demanded.

Alma sighed. "How many guests? A hundred?"

He spoke expansively. "Five hundred!"

But he felt deflated. The boy was a bad omen, a spectre who meant him no good.

He grumbled to himself and crossed the room. His bandy legs, short for his girth, bowed beneath the belly's weight. His spine angled backwards, slumping away from the belly, sinking into the tiny backside; his head lolled forward. In silhouette he resembled a lower case g. The boy, he thought. His only son, his child. Thirty hours in delivery. Unwilling to exit from Alma's stomach, the boy had resisted life, preferring the darkness. Well, who could blame him?

"I want the boy at the party."

She hesitated.

"Don't stammer. I said I want him!"

"He starts college tomorrow. He'll be away at college."

"He can come to his old man's party."

She sighed. "Not to show him off. Not an exhibit."

"That's not my reason!"

He tilted his large head and reflected. "Ah, what fun! We'll sing. The old songs. All the old boys singing together. What harmonies! What a grand thing, the dear boys. The old gang." His spirits lifted. He performed an awkward clog

15

step, then clasped his hands before him. As Alma smiled patiently at his flushed face, he opened his mouth so wide his gold fillings reflected the chandelier's light. A pure tenor emerged, thin and airy, surprisingly light and wistful, untrained but diligent:

"I've got a white man driving my automobile.
And when my money runs out, I'll steal.
Just to keep that white man driving my auto-mo—
Driving my auto-mobile."

She stood beside him, a half-inch shorter. He clasped her waist and began again as her alto rose a third above his tenor and contributed a tentative harmony to his rendition of "Second Hand Rose."

Midway through the song, he tickled her. She ran from him, laughing. He circled her body with his arms.

"I remember the night we heard Fanny Brice sing that song. She could break your heart."

He released his wife and said soberly, "Fanny Brice was a great artist. I never played for the great ones. Only the strippers and pansy baritones."

"You'll play at the party. They'll insist on it."

"They better. It's my booze and food. You know, it's funny. We're both musical and the boy can't sing a note."

"He's an artist," she explained.

"Some artist!"

"He is," she replied.

"What do you know about it?"

"Nothing. But if that's what he wants . . ."

A knock startled Aaron. With a look of surprise, his parents opened his door and stood restlessly.

His father spoke: "What are you working on?"

"Paintings."

"Well, well."

"Yes," he said expansively. "That's what I'm working on."

"You could have fooled me."

His mother observed him critically. "That's no way to make an impression."

Sol entered the room and busied himself peering behind the stacks of pictures. He squatted to take a closer look and grunted.

"They're all naked!"

Aaron frowned.

"Tell me something. Why do you paint only naked women?"

He fixed his son with a slow, benign tilt of his large head, and cigar ash spilled on his belly. His salesman's smile preceding his genial voice: as if for the first time, he suggested to Aaron that he cancel his plans for college and begin work the following Monday. After a few years, in which to get the hang of things, he would commence his inevitable takeover of the management of the Company.

The news surprised Alma. "He's only nineteen," she protested.

"I started work at twelve. It was no picnic."

"Times are different."

"He's got a head on his shoulders."

"He needs an education!"

"He's educated!"

Sol removed his cigar and delicately balanced it on the edge of the windowsill. He sat in a chair; he patted his big stomach and slid far down into his chair; he regarded Aaron with his eyes just above the level of the boy's chest.

"You turned out better than I figured. You're nineteen. Everything's going to be O.K."

He folded his hands over his stomach and peacefully sucked a stray bit of tobacco between his teeth.

"At your age—with your life ahead of you. You'll start at seventy-five dollars a week. And your own car. Tomorrow we'll go to Balding's. Buy you a car. You're a lucky kid. Live at home. No expenses. The seventy-five is all yours. . . .

"It's a dog-eat-dog world. You got to slug it out toe to toe. . . .

"I'll make it eighty-five a week and ten dollars expenses. Write your own ticket."

Aaron said, "It's my life."

"Think it over. You'll spend four more years in college. You'll sing and drink. In two years you can be married with children of your own and making two thousand a month!"

"Who's he going to marry, for God's sake!" Alma's voice rose in pursuit.

"Everybody gets married! Let me ask you something. What kind of a person takes off her clothes?"

"Models."

"For strangers?"

"Listen," Aaron said, "you'll have to excuse me. I want to work now."

"Of course. Paint naked people."

Alma said, "Leave him alone."

Sol patted Aaron's back. He grinned at him. "I'll see you tomorrow. In the morning. Otis will take you to the station."

"If you don't mind, I'm going alone. I'll say goodbye now."

"Who'll take you to the train?"

"I'll manage."

Sol bit hard on his cigar and complained: "You'll manage!"

Alma said, "Try to be nice. Tomorrow he's going to college."

"I'll say goodbye, old-timer. Stay out of trouble. Keep your mouth shut and your fly buttoned." He held out his hand and Aaron shook it.

"Goodbye."

"Goodbye, old-timer."

Alma folded her arms. "Fathers and sons should kiss," she explained. "It's not terrible."

Sol removed his cigar and faced his son; they stood warily, like experts in judo; they circled. The kiss landed unspent in the space between them.

3

THE NEXT MORNING, in a triplex on the East Seventies, Helga Fern packed every bit of clothing. Preparatory to her trip to college, she arranged twelve suitcases and a steamer trunk in the center of her bedroom and waited for the arrival of her mother, whose imminent appearance caused such waves of self-pity, she sighed with nausea. She slumped to her bed, a clumsy Viking of a girl who lumbered through life and avoided mirrors. Her mutinous expression spoiled what might have been a pretty face, her hockey player's legs caused no second glances, and her greenish-blond metallic hair was cut just short of masculinity.

Troubled, she touched her cold sore. She draped a lavender sweater over her head and blinked beneath the dark, soft tent as high-heeled shoes pounded the hallway and disturbed the crystal on the overhead chandelier.

Her door opened with a violent thrust and banged against the closet wall.

"Sit up."

Corliss Fern charged the room in a sleeveless dress from

Henri Bendel. Unruffled and backed by eight generations of old money and friends in high places, she greeted her daughter.

"What's it to be? Lollygagging?"

Helga slumped.

Through the open door, Simpson, the white sheep dog, padded in, hesitated, then moved serenely toward Helga, who instantly dropped to her knees to embrace and kiss his head.

"You're a dear chap."

Corliss jerked her arms like a bandmaster. Her staccato voice chopped the air. "I'm not impressed."

Helga released the dog. "When you pack your clothes for college, you should, you know, be left alone by people, and you should be permitted a little peace."

"If you've packed without consulting me, you're in for a surprise."

"People should trust you. Especially if you're old enough to pack your own things."

"Where is the key?"

"People should have privacy. It's vital."

Corliss clapped her hands together. "Thank heaven your father's not alive to hear this!"

Helga blew her nose. "Leave him out of this. You married him."

"Married him!"

"People should stop saying he's dead. He's only sixty-one."

"A corpse!"

Helga sobbed. "Mothers and daughters should love each other."

Corliss tentatively kicked at a suitcase. She slapped it with her open hand.

"You can't be trusted to pack yourself!" She flung open a

large brown suitcase and pulled out a pair of bell-bottomed blue jeans.

"Heavens!" She threw them on the floor. She removed three cotton sweatshirts, some green sneakers, and a stack of men's button-down shirts. She dropped to her knees and attacked another bag.

Vernon Fern appeared, standing in the open doorway, his hands in the jacket of his dressing robe.

"Why are you thrashing so? Can't the maids do that?" He considered the pile of clothing.

His wife glared at the stuff about her.

"I was saying, Cor, why can't servants attend to that mess?" He touched his moustache. "Good morning, Helga."

She answered glumly, "Hello."

Corliss said, "Git!"

Vernon smiled pleasantly. "We're waiting breakfast."

"We're packing!"

"Ah, packing."

His son Toby loomed behind him in an identical silk dressing gown. He was six and a half feet tall, with a tiny-featured handsome face and the solemnity of a weight lifter.

"Mom. Dad. Helga. Morning. . . . Breakfast?"

Vernon poked him on the arm. "My very question."

Helga impotently hit her fists together as her mother resumed her attack on the clothing, churning and clawing and tugging at dresses, stockings, and sweaters.

"To begin with, you have more than you'll ever find use for. You're going to college, not a safari."

Vernon chuckled and examined his wife. She seemed overtired.

"I have a migraine," she informed him.

"Now, now. We're all edgy."

"Get me aspirin. I never wanted children."

"Now, now, Cor."

"It feels like a tumor."

The dog leaped backwards and barked. Vernon pulled his son into the room and shut the door behind them. "The servants." He strode to the window and turned his back on his family. He peered down at East 72nd Street, then out towards the heavy autumn foliage of Central Park; children and nannies walked dogs beneath his window.

"Well," he said hopelessly. "This strife and torment. And our girl going off to college. Let's leave the packing. I'll ice a bottle."

Someone knocked.

"Yes?" Vernon walked across the room to open it.

Agnes peeked in fearfully. "Cook suggests breakfast is ready."

Corliss smiled. "How do you expect me to eat?"

Toby prepared to leave. "I'm going down to breakfast."

"Wait for your mother." Vernon took Corliss' arm and helped her to her feet. "Has the pain eased?"

"A little!"

In single file, Corliss leading, they proceeded down the hallway, past the Bonnards and Vuillards that comprised part of Vernon's collection and onto the marble stairway to the entrance hall that led to the dining room. There, under a chandelier that once hung in Versailles, they seated themselves and lowered their heads.

"We thank thee, Father, for all thy blessings." Vernon said grace conversationally. "We're especially pleased with your attitude towards Helga, who will, with your help, do marvelously well at college, the same school, you know, that her mother and her mother's mother attended. We are equally grateful for your intercession in the case of Toby, who apparently is doing so well at his insurance business he's in line for some sort of promotion. Watch over him, Father, he's a perfectly swell boy who should get on in this world. Please bless this house, and my wife Corliss, and this food and the servants. Thanks again. Amen."

Two maids entered, carrying pewter trays.

Toby drank a tankard of orange juice and grinned at his sister. Helga opened her napkin with the patience of a soldier unfolding the American flag. When the food reached her, she removed from the tray three fried eggs, a half pound of bacon and seven slices of cinnamon toast, placing each item with geometric precision on her plate before commencing the laborious task of cutting, spreading, and chewing.

Corliss sipped tea. She watched her children digest. She stood up. She excused herself by informing them it was time.

"We're going shopping!"

Corliss brushed her hair, powdered her pale face, put on carmine lipstick, and explained crisply that although she was in considerable pain, she would go to the station. "Since you've made a mess of your packing, I've instructed Agnes to fix an overnight bag for you. We'll shop now."

Helga flushed. She looked for allies, but her father involved himself in lighting his cigarette, and Toby stared at the chandelier.

"There, there," Vernon said. He stood and walked towards his daughter. "Don't you fret, dear."

He placed an arm about Helga's shoulders and kissed her cheek. "I'll say goodbye, dear girl."

Toby held out his large hand. "So long, Hellie," he said formally. "See you."

She shook his hand, nodded, and struggled with her tears.

Agnes appeared, carrying a small overnight bag.

"Goodbye, miss. Have a nice time at the college."

Corliss, who wore a tan cashmere over her sleeveless

dress, was ready. She handed her daughter a white raincoat and pointed towards the front door.

They left together without speaking. In the outer hall, Pat, the elevator man, waited. They entered his car. "Lovely day."

Corliss agreed.

He pushed the main floor button, and they descended.

Helga was a six-foot woman, Corliss was barely five feet; together they made an odd pair, shopping side by side on Fifth Avenue.

"There, that's nice," Corliss said, plucking at Helga's sleeve. "There! Right there!" She indicated a store window in the Fifties.

Helga complained, "People shouldn't pluck at each other," and dragged her arm back. Corliss darted into the store and engaged a salesgirl before Helga shuffled through the entrance. "For my daughter."

Helga grumbled. "People's taste is not always the same."

"Nonsense. The very thing. Bring me one in white. Bring me one in tan."

Helga catalogued the injustices she had suffered that day at her mother's side.

Morosely, she stood aside listening to her mother instruct the salesgirl with the firm tone of authority: a quiet alto.

"No," she said. "Not that one, that one . . . the blue one. . . . And the shirt . . . I like a gray shirt. . . . It's so . . . serviceable." She touched and rubbed and plucked the fabric. She held it to the light. She pointed, checked the sizes, and peered and poked and burrowed into the pile of clothing and chose three shirts, two blouses, and a cashmere cardigan. "Wrap them. We'll take them," she said, "and hurry."

Helga formed her large hands into fists and stood like a sentinel, her arms straight at her sides, her high square shoulders stiff with protest. She watched resentfully as the salesgirl arranged the clothing in a pile and said, "There's a dressing room in the rear." Gathering up the things in her arms, she advanced towards it.

"No, no," Corliss said airily. "No time to try them on. We're leaving for college in a very few hours. That is, she is. If they don't fit properly, we'll exchange them."

Helga resisted an impulse to sweep out her large hand and knock the whole lot onto the floor. Instead, she sullenly waited as the girl wrapped the package.

"There's Craig now," Corliss said, waving and pointing toward a Rolls Royce. The chauffeur pulled the car to the curb, parked it, and entered the store. He gathered the packages and silently returned to the car.

Corliss paid three hundred and twelve dollars by check and exited. Helga followed.

Out on the street they continued, her mother darting ahead looking in windows, Helga remaining a few paces behind, muttering, while Craig shepherded them both in the family Rolls, keeping close to curbs. Corliss skipped and gestured vivaciously, while Helga moved like someone on snowshoes.

When they were about to enter a second store, Helga stopped. She gazed down and spoke in a halting tone, as if she were breaking a code. "People go too far." She loomed in the doorway and cast a brooding shadow over the sweaters displayed in the shop window. Her wide face was flat with despair. Her eyes brimmed with tears. Her somber mouth, a sad line of discontent, pouted helplessly. She was nineteen years old, she explained. A woman, practically. Not a pet.

Corliss gazed up. She saw the familiar depressed look of a movie Indian, the wide Seminole face of her only child. Why, she wondered, was I given this huge halfback of a daughter instead of the children one sees in the ads? She patted Helga's wrist. "Come into the car, dear."

"How many sweaters should a person own?"

"One can't have too many sweaters if one perspires."

Helga regarded her mother with hatred. She considered toppling on her like a huge somnolent oak.

"When you're in college, dear, you will do as you wish. While you're in my care, buy what I tell you." She smiled winsomely, blinked, and stepped smartly into the Rolls Royce. She opened her purse and freshened her lipstick. "My," she said, pursing and working her lips together. "I envy you, child. What a gay adventure, going to college. What times you'll have. I remember my college days. All the young men! Dinners at the Plaza. Regatta week. The dances. The balls. We danced and drank too much champagne and saw the sun come up and hugged each other and congratulated ourselves on being so young and being attractive. Goodness me, we *were* an attractive bunch. Dudley and your father and Pinky Potter and Sally Lang, Cynthia Baxton, Muggsy Phipps. Vital people." She paused and touched her daughter's cheek. "You can be that too, dear. Many beautiful people are unattractive. But if your soul is clean and you have a sweetness, people respond to you as surely as if you were a movie star. I know. I was never a beauty. Not like Sylvia Neal or the Livingston twins, but I had my share. Young men noticed me. Your father danced every dance with me the night we met. He was so smitten he tore up my dance card and ate the pieces for fear some other lads would claim their dances."

Helga considered fainting.

"I wore my hair short then. A flapper, you might say."

"Not me." Helga spoke darkly. "Too tall for boys, too gloomy for girls, too depressed for social work . . ."

Corliss laughed. "It's not true in the least."

"... A freak. An outcast!"

"You must fight self-pity with all your strength."

"A figure out of Stonehenge. A Cardiff giant." She slumped so far forward her knees rested on the back of the chauffeur's seat.

"Merely large. Not a giant. Blow your nose, wipe your eyes. Goodness! As a child you wore braces and moped and didn't share. You pushed smaller children in front of swings, threw sand, threw up, crossed streets, caught cold, used your sleeve, wouldn't listen, wouldn't nap. Change! My goodness, you've sulked enough! Nineteen years!"

"You're sending me away. To college."

Corliss shook her head with dismay. "As a child you rarely smiled except in triumph, if someone fell or lost a glove. Be patient. God will find you. He found me early. I was cheerful the instant I saw His world. This lovely place. God's lovely world."

Helga arched her back so that her neck lay flat on the seat. From this position, below the window, her eyes gazed mournfully at the ceiling. "When God gives someone one hundred and seventy pounds of unwarranted flesh, it's difficult to love Him."

"He loves you even if you harden your heart to Him."

"No He doesn't. A frog, quiet and numb on a lily pad, notices me and sinks to the bottom. The brave sounds of morning: birds, dogs, rabbits. They see me and clam up!"

"What do you want?"

"Oblivion. No one dances with a Watusi. Too clumsy for sports. Prepared for nothing. A no-man's-land. Limbo. Unwanted, shunned, and despised." She nodded knowledgeably. "Tall girls could teach Jesus."

"Don't blaspheme!"

"Don't shout at people!"

They heard a knock at the car window. They looked up to see Aaron Franklin peering in and smiling. He was burdened with boxes and shopping bags. An easel was strapped to his back. A pile of suitcases was arranged at his feet. His face and hair were wet with perspiration.

Helga warned, "Don't open the window."

The chauffeur turned to them for instruction.

Corliss said, "He's just a boy," and cautiously lowered the window.

"Thank you," he said. "It's been some morning."

"What do you want?"

"I want to thank you for opening your window. No one has even done that."

"I see."

"There's an amazing amount of fear around."

He mopped his forehead with a paisley handkerchief, shifted the weight of the easel from his left to his right shoulder, and explained himself. "My name is Aaron Franklin." He replaced the handkerchief in the breast pocket of his tweed jacket and smiled pleasantly.

He continued. "No bus will accept me. Taxis see me and go off duty. I'm leaving for Burton College on the eleven-ten from Grand Central. I want to get this equipment on the train with me. I hope you'll be kind enough to help me. I've been in the sun on this corner for an hour and my train leaves so soon I doubt if I'll make it without your help."

Corliss said, "You want to store that gear in my automobile?"

"That's it!"

"Certainly not."

"I'm overextended." He peered into the dark rear seat.

From the front seat the chauffeur said: "Go away."

But he continued, leaning forward, speaking conversationally into the darkness. "This easel is made of oak. My suitcases are filled with art supplies."

Finally from inside the limousine he heard a clear deep voice. "Are you still speaking to me, young fellow?"

"That's right."

"I'll have the driver deal with you."

He pleaded with her. "You have room back there." He shifted the weight on his back amid creaking of leather straps. He remained standing, grinning foolishly.

The car started down the street, leaving him leaning forward like a hod carrier. He lurched a few feet after the car, then collapsed backward as the weight of the easel pulled him to the side, and in struggling to remain standing, he fell onto his suitcases. The tennis racket slid to the gutter.

4

THE TRAIN WAS RAPIDLY FILLING with young people. Aaron looked about benignly.

The car grew thick with gesticulating students, most of whom wore sweaters beneath their sunburned faces. The train started.

A girl in a black raincoat sat across the aisle. Her black disorderly hair fell in a thick fold above her eyebrows. Her rapt face startled him. Her superior eyes gazed inward as if to say: No one is trustworthy.

The conductor tapped his arm and asked for his ticket. He produced it, had it punched, and looked back to the girl who had changed her position. She searched for a ticket in her handbag as the conductor approached. When she turned, she noticed him staring. Her eyes widened and held his momentarily.

She hid her breasts behind a fashion magazine, fondling it like an accordion.

Bracing himself against the shake and rock of the train, he considered her. It was, he felt, like a popular song. Their eyes met. They held each other like eyes in a mirror. Her body straightened and leaned toward him. His face ached from the wideness of his smile. She smiled, too, briefly.

The older man (her father?) noticed him. He was an inelegant fellow with a soft look and a carnation in his lapel. He turned in his seat to address Aaron.

"Heading for Burton?"

Aaron smothered his smile and nodded.

"Ah."

Aaron marveled at her body. He blinked. He was aware of her father unwinding, like a rusted piece of machinery. He creaked and rustled his tweed-jacketed arm until it extended into the aisle.

Aaron shook his hand. "I'm new," he explained.

"How do you do. I am Gus Gang. My daughter is a student. Name of Polly."

He shrugged and sat straight in his chair.

Her father spoke. "See by your gear, you're a painter."

Aaron nodded.

"Why are you staring at my daughter?"

Aaron lowered his head.

"Going to the club car now." He brushed past his daughter and eased himself into the aisle. He fixed Aaron with a suspicious look and admonished him: "Mind your P's and Q's."

Her father walked toward the front of the car.

He continued staring at her. When she began reading her magazine, he cleared his throat. She looked up.

"What is it?"

"I'd like to talk to you."

She frowned.

He insisted. "I mean it."

She sighed.

32

"Do you go to movies?"

"Yes." She talked directly into her magazine.

"I only see foreign films. I just go for the subtitles. I block out the top three-quarters of the screen with my hand and figure out the plot from the subtitles."

She regarded him with surprise.

"Everyone should be subtitled. You wouldn't watch their mouths. Only their stomachs."

Her expression softened. She seemed ready to talk as, shifting in her seat, she faced him and said exploratorily, "How tall are you?"

"I'd like to dub my parents."

"I asked you a question."

"I'm well over six feet. I slouch."

Tilting her head, she tapped her chin with one finger. "Don't you have a name?" she asked.

"Aaron Franklin. I'm a painter." He glanced quickly down the aisle, then indicated the spot her father had vacated. "I wonder if I could sit with you."

"That's my father's seat."

"He won't be back. He went for a drink."

She hesitated.

"Does he drink a lot?"

She nodded.

He said, "My father is so angry, he made a million dollars."

"Don't you like him?"

"Sure."

She leaned closer. "Why do you want to sit over here?"

"You're a beautiful girl."

"You just met me."

"I've rarely seen such a beautiful person."

He shifted his suitcases and pictures and awkwardly

33

pushed himself to his feet, where, balancing against the swaying train, he stood over her and asked again.

"You actually think I should?" she said.

When he moved past her, holding himself erect and proper, he felt the warmth of her nyloned legs against his pants and considered stumbling into her lap. Instead he moved discreetly past her knees and seated himself. He stared at her. She blushed. He felt his own cheeks grow warm and decided that perhaps he loved her. He relaxed beside her.

"You're a first-rate girl."

She laughed nervously. "I am?"

"I'll tell the world!"

He felt a hand on his shoulder.

"You're in my seat, young man."

The girl said, "Hello, Daddy."

Aaron turned. Her father, his full face gray behind his soft nose, stood over him.

"I am back! Polly, ask him to get up."

"Get up," she said.

5

HE REMAINED IN THE MEN'S ROOM until the train stopped. He smoked a cigar and grimaced at himself in the mirror. There was no doubting it. Love had caught him unawares.

When the train stopped at the Poughkeepsie station, he raised the shade and peered out the window, hoping to see her. Students were leaping at each other on the station platform. They laughed in the hot September sunshine. Porters were unloading suitcases and packing cases from the train and carrying them to waiting buses. Boys and girls surrounded each other, hands were shaken in boisterous greeting, but she wasn't there.

He turned from the window, unbolted the door, and stepped into the aisle. The car was almost empty: the girl and her father were gone. He quickly ran to his seat and gathered his things.

Warily guarding his possessions, elbows out like a basketball player, he made his slow way down the aisle and laboriously navigated the three iron steps. On the ground he lowered his head, spread his legs, and stared out defiantly, shielding his things from the milling mob of students.

A porter advanced, his face damp from exertion. Aaron eyed him suspiciously. He shook his head and held out his hand. "Get back," he said. The porter shrugged and moved away, making a circular motion with his finger at his ear.

Suspicious of the school bus, he found a taxi near the station. Slouching on the back seat he smoked a new cigar and wondered where the girl had gone and if her heart like his was beating faster.

"Here we are, sonny." The driver indicated two iron gates on the left of the highway.

The noise was deafening. The first-day excitement astounded him. Reunited friends clapped each other's backs. Horns sounded. He blinked. He retreated behind a tree and took inventory. A tall boy tapped his arm.

"I'm on the welcoming committee."

"I'm Aaron Franklin. I'm new."

"You play basketball?"

"No."

"That's all right."

Aaron whispered, "You could help me. . . . How can I find a new student? Her name is Polly Gang."

The boy pointed to a large white frame building in front of which many students talked and gestured noisily and jumped about in colorful profusion.

"That's Bodkin Hall. The main building. New students must register there."

"I'll go and wait for her."

He stepped back as, squinting into the sun, he tried to locate her in the mob of faces. He entered the building and, after a long delay, was assigned a room in the men's dormitory. He went outside and waited.

"Hi," she said shyly. He swung about. She stood next to him.

"Where have you been?" he demanded. "I've been looking for you."

She stared at the ground. "I want you to leave me alone. My father doesn't like you."

She had removed her black raincoat. She stood before him in a plaid skirt, a pink cardigan sweater above which a dickey showed like an envelope flap.

"Where's your father?" he asked.

"He's with Mr. Mindlin, the president. They're schoolmates."

"He's quick to take offense."

"It's hard for him. I'm his only child."

"We can't talk here." He took her arm. "We'll take a walk together."

She pulled away. "You aren't the first boy. It's happened before. It's something about me. Boys come up. Total strangers."

"I don't blame them."

"It's hard on him. My father."

"You're the girl for me."

"Now stop that! Honestly. What's your game?"

"Why don't you walk with me?"

"I can't. You don't know how it is for a father when he has a popular daughter. I'm all he has."

"What about your mother?"

She spoke softly. "She's very sick."

"I'm sorry."

"She's dying, I think."

"Why isn't he with her?"

"Because."

"Because why?"

37

"You wouldn't understand."

She suddenly sat on the grass, cross-legged. She clenched her fists and spoke slowly.

"It's terribly hard, being a girl. Boys have it much easier."

"Then, let's take a walk."

"My father will be looking."

"Forget him." He pointed to a far-off hill. "No one will miss us."

He placed his arm around her shoulders and said in a comradely manner, "We'll just talk. We can be great friends."

She pulled away. He quickly took her arm and tugged her to him.

Her face paled. "Don't! Don't make trouble."

He showed her the men's dormitory. "We'll meet behind that building. In two minutes. You go first." When she hesitated, he gently propelled her forward.

He found her behind the building.

She allowed him to direct her across a wide lawn.

Near the football field, he said, "My paintings! I forgot them."

"Nobody will steal them."

He kicked at a pebble. "They're valuable."

They came upon a stream, barely visible in the heavy autumn foliage.

He guided her along the mossy bank until the stream curved into the dense woods and they were out of view.

In a conversational tone that disguised his confusion, he asked her how she felt.

"It's cool here."

Their proximity frightened him. Suddenly feeling feverish, he suggested they stop. This must be love, he thought as, staring into her eyes, he felt such longing for her that he blinked.

He tensed his arms and, stiff as a marionette, placed his hand on her shoulder. "Have you ever been in love?"

"Don't be dumb."

He wet his lips. He looked at her pretty face and smelled her perfume. He felt overcome by a sweet sensation and the thrust of his swollen hopes, he lunged for her and hugged her.

Rather like a wrestler than a lover, he held her desperately for fear the life would run out of him.

She admonished him. "What are you doing?"

He released her, his legs vibrating with such ferocity he seated himself on the moss and, fascinated, watched them tremble.

"Look at that," he exclaimed. "Isn't that marvelous?"

They performed a shaky tap dance, quivered, and lay still. The tic spread. It jerked at his shoulder causing his arm to flail and flop about like a fish. From a staccato beat to a shuddering quiver, his palsied hand thrashed at the ground.

She removed her moccasins and stepped into the water. She picked her way upstream, jumping from stone to stone, executing each leap gracefully despite the slippery moss.

She returned, splashing at the water and sprinkling her face. "I love the country. We stayed in the city all summer. Mother was sick and we had to be near the hospital."

She seated herself next to him and traced circles on the ground with her fingernail. She stretched and yawned.

"We'd better go back. Daddy will be worried."

He threw his arms about her. Instead of resisting, he felt her body press on his, humming and vibrating like a motor. They rocked and rubbed against each other. She held him in a grip of iron. She squeezed him, he squeezed her. Suddenly his legs began to tremble. He shook and danced like a minstrel and then, without warning, overflowed and astonished himself as, hanging on for fear he'd buckle, an ocean of pleasure softened his body and he released her and leaned against her gratefully and doubted if his father had ever felt such exquisite joy.

She drew back. "We'd better stop."

He agreed.

She straightened her sweater and put on her moccasins. "I'll go first. You wait. Then it won't look suspicious."

He took her hand and they walked back together.

Near a clump of trees on the outer edge of the campus, Gus Gang shielded his eyes and watched them approach. He waved when he saw them and called, "Polly! Over here. Hurry!" He held a yellow piece of paper in his hand. He appeared to be in pain.

"Daddy," she said. "What is it?"

He jabbed at the dust with his shoe. "I'm afraid it's bad."

She ran to him. He placed his arms about her and drew her close. "I received a telegram. It's your mother."

Aaron said brightly, "Can I help?"

"She's much worse."

Polly gasped.

"Yes," he said coughing, his eyes filling with tears. "In fact, she's dying. Poor woman, all alone."

"Oh, Daddy," Polly wailed. She clutched him. They embraced.

Aaron shoved his hands in his pockets and waited uncomfortably.

Gus Gang's pleading eyes gazed at him above his daughter's head. "This is personal."

He released his daughter and blew his nose.

As Aaron attempted to comfort her, she said, "Get back."

"So that's how it is!"

"It's Daddy. I must take care of him."

"Daughters don't take care of fathers. Fathers look after daughters."

"He needs me."

"How about me?"

Aaron moved away and observed them from a distance.

Arm in arm they walked toward the taxicab. As they entered, Polly turned to him and waved mournfully.

"Goodbye. It was nice meeting you."

He rushed to her. "What do you mean? It wasn't nice! It was an event! An epiphany." He leaned into the cab window and shouted at her, "You can't leave me now."

"I'll be back."

He tore at the handle of the door. "I'll come too!"

Gus said, "Get him away."

"He's only trying to help," she said.

"Polly! Mother is dying! She may be breathing her last breath on this earth."

"He's right, Aaron. There's nothing you can do. I mean it. You're sweet, but what can you do?"

Gus signaled the driver to start. The car drove off.

6

AARON HESITATED before the dormitory door. He set his paintings and his suitcases down. Inside, Helga Fern was bending over his bed. A scrub brush, a bucket, and a mop and broom lay on the floor beside her as she hummed and tugged at his blanket.

"Hello," he said.

Helga raised her head and regarded him sideways. "I'm the maid." She wore the unjolly look of domestic workers. "Is this your room?"

"It is. I'm Franklin."

"People aren't always maids."

He examined her. A pale yellow bandana clasped the rollers in her hair. A too-large seersucker dress hung loosely from her wide shoulders, its missing top buttons exposing much of her breasts. She had rolled the sleeves back on her muscular arms.

As he continued to stare, she pushed herself back from the bed and stood erect. He marveled. She was at least a six-foot woman. She raised one arm and, reaching behind her, scratched her shoulder blade.

"People do things for the money," she said.

He was about to speak when she langorously turned and bent over. Her wide seersucker backside loomed up from the bed as she straightened the edge of the sheet. Then she turned towards him.

She fell forward on the bed, lying on her stomach, her face in the pillow.

"Maybe I should leave. I'll come back." He stared at her haunches.

She rolled over, her arms folded over her breasts. She forced herself to her feet and, taking up the broom, commenced sweeping.

He examined the room. It was high-ceilinged and narrow. Leaded windows filled one wall and looked out onto the rear of the campus. The other walls were blank and damp as a cell. A large empty desk, a leather easy chair, and the single bed had a film of dust from her sweeping. He backed out into the hall saying, "I'll be back."

But as he turned, she said, "How tall are you?" She was leaning on her broom like a laborer on a shovel. Before he could respond she added, "You hate this job!"

"I do?"

"No. People hate it."

He agreed.

"It's not someone's cup of tea," she said. "It's minority work." She slumped heavily into the chair, the broom resting against her legs. "When you're nineteen, it's not like you're thirty or forty."

"You're a strange maid," he said.

She looked depressed. "It's a question of money." She wiped her mouth with her large hand. "You do fourteen rooms in this dormitory every other day. You change sheets once a week on every bed. Not the bathroom, however. Imagine walking in on somebody or other in the bathroom." She turned her face up and stared remotely at the blank wall. "How do you like college?"

He explained he didn't know. He had just arrived.

"College is a thorough tragedy," she said. "It corrupts."

"You talk a lot for nineteen."

She lowered her head to complain: "That's not particularly nice."

The small room seemed hot and close. He considered opening the window. Instead, he closed the door behind him.

She glumly chewed her knuckles. "You can bruise yourself cleaning."

For the past few minutes his heart had been pounding; now, with the door shut, his knees trembled.

"Are all maids like you?"

She gazed suspiciously. "No one cares if you bruise yourself. It hurts. Mother laughs herself sick whenever you stumble. As a child, people had awful parents."

"Everyone does."

She smoothed her dress over her muscular legs, crossed her large, sneakered feet, and hummed to herself. He stood above her, his shirt sticking to him; sweat from his forehead stung his eyes. Outside, the sound of students and car horns could be faintly heard.

"This room is done."

"It looks pretty dirty to me," he said tensely. He rubbed his finger on the desk top. "You call this clean?"

"It's a shame the way they work people. It's not as if you're some ignoramus."

"You'd better stay and clean this room."

She undid the remaining buttons on her dress and fanned

herself with the material, exposing a pink brassiere that seized the bottoms of her disproportionately small breasts. She stood and moved towards the bed where she sat and described her ailments.

"You get severe cramps and migraine headaches. The pain is unendurable. You simply faint to escape."

Her defeated eyes intrigued him. He examined her long, downturned mouth, her tiny eyes, her pale, perplexed eyebrows. Beneath the bandana, her lifeless blond hair, hidden by hooplike metallic rollers, tugged at the freckled skin on her forehead, lending a quizzical look to her Eskimo face. She resembled women in the roller derby.

She placed one foot on top of the other, leaned forward allowing him an unobstructed view, and said mournfully, "Had Father's people lived, they wouldn't be here. They'd be in the south of Spain. Or some place. If your father chased you with a shotgun when you were seven years old, and once hit your mother so hard she was unconscious for a good part of the afternoon, you'd feel odd. When he wasn't drinking, he slept around. He parted his hair in the middle and sang like Russ Columbo. He wore double-breasted suits and forty-dollar shoes while people did without. Mother was a famous actress before she married him. He made her give it up. They were happy together. Then one day, love flew out the window." She laughed tonelessly.

Outside, a bell rang four times. He wondered how long he could stand still without going towards her. He locked the door and waited. She sat with her elbows on her knees, supporting her chin on her hands; her pale neck shone with perspiration.

He stepped closer and placed his hand on her hard shoulder. She pulled away.

"Don't," she said.

"Sorry," he said, keeping his hand on her.

"Don't you hear?"

"I said I was sorry."

"Then remove your hand."

"All right," he said.

He squeezed the back of her neck and dragged his hand down her arm. At the elbow, he slid off and pressed his fingers against her stomach. She was quite strong. She gripped his wrist with one hand and shoved him away. He regained his balance and reached for her. This time, as he squeezed her arm, she looked at him as though the arm belonged to someone else. She showed no emotion, so he let go and breathed deeply and started again. He held her shoulders in both hands and forced her back. The realization of what he was doing darkened her face.

"You there!" she barked and shot forward, freeing herself with one fast shove. "Mustn't push people about," she warned, shaking her finger.

He sat on the edge of the desk behind her. She stood, her dress hanging loosely, her bandana askew. She kicked her sneaker off and, placing her hands on her hips, her thick legs apart, she faced him glumly and said, "Some people are no pushovers."

He sprang from the desk and butted his shoulders into her stomach, wrapping his arms around her as he did. Hanging on desperately, he twisted her onto the bed. She fought back, thrashing her great legs and heaving her shoulders. Her bandana flew off as did half her curlers. She managed to get a knee under his chest and propelled him off her. But he shifted his weight, redoubled his pursuit, and slowly gained control. She grunted and struggled, but his surprise attack gave him a slight advantage and he placed his knees on her shoulders as she fought beneath him.

Deciding to end it, she relaxed her body, unclenched her fists, and said with dignity, "Get off."

"You're strong," he said, adding with sincerity, "as a man."

Her curlers banged painfully on his forehead as she butted him with her head, arched her body, and flung him up with a burst of fury and wild energy. Punching at his neck and shoulders, she locked her legs about him and twisted him over. Instantly, she was on her feet, gasping and coughing, her threatening hand raised in a theatrical gesture.

"Don't ever say that! People hate that."

He rubbed his forehead, which felt damp with sweat. A slow trickle of blood ran down his arm onto the pillow.

"What gives you the right to grab at someone?" She frowned and shrugged her shoulders and slumped into the chair, saying darkly, "It's not your fault. However," she added defensively, "it's hard work being a maid in this heat." She buttoned her dress and rearranged her curlers, one of which, having rolled partially down her cheek, rested against her nose.

He said, "Lighten my prison."

"Why?"

"That's Baudelaire."

She grunted. "People should communicate. They shouldn't rush at people." She crossed her legs and said, pleasantly, "What are your hopes?"

He rubbed his face. His arms ached, as did his neck.

She said, "My father gave his money away to passersby because he wanted love. We were willing to give him love, but he wasn't able to receive it." She gazed dumbly at her feet.

She was reaching inside her dress to straighten her brassiere when he leaped at her, but she was quick. She was on her feet and up on the ledge that ran beneath the leaded windows, her large frame blocking the light, resembling an enormous bird in silhouette, and he found himself sprawled in the vacated chair, his arms embracing the warm leather, his chin hanging over the back.

She yelled at him. "That's enough!"

He agreed. "You can come down now."

"If someone wants something of someone, they should ask, not grab." She leaped down, landing with a thud that shook the room. She primped her bandana, lowered her head, and shyly reported to him, "All you have to do is ask someone."

"I'm asking."

"Do you want to do it? I mean here?"

He nodded.

"I guessed as much. Pull down the shades."

He did, the room was completely dark and in the darkness he heard her wrestling with her buttons, heard her step out of her dress, pull back the sheets, and climb into bed.

He pulled off his clothes and, groping his way towards the bed, located her head. He jumped in beside her and hugged her hard body.

"I'm glad I'm here," he said and grabbed for her breasts. They felt strangely soft and meaningless. He rubbed them. He twisted them gently as if they were dials. He lowered his hands down her stomach. At her navel, he paused. She hadn't moved. She lay joyless and patient. He searched for her lips with his mouth and cut his chin on the edge of a curler as she turned her head sideways.

"I don't kiss," she informed him. "It's not one of my things."

His hand returned to her stomach. It probed, patted, tickled, and plucked.

He manipulated, entered and massaged her, investigating

every shadow, crevice, and indentation. He clinched and speculated. He wandered all over her territory, feeling removed, cut off from life like a surveyor in an unfamiliar district. He cleared his throat in protest, sensing the war had passed him by, a soldier far behind the enemy lines, searching the hedgerows and orchards for his company.

"I'm not wearing anything," she explained, her voice far below him from some cistern.

Disengaged, his clutch gone, his accelerator jammed, he sped an entire speedway, passing the Lotus and three Ferraris without a single pit stop.

Then, he climbed down and lay beside her, sensing her reproachful silence; the hot room swelled with the remorse, injustice, and the martyrdom of her voice.

"Why were you so rough?"

Justifying himself, he said, "You must get to the net! You stay in the back court, hitting deep backhands, you'll never break through. Even if you have to force yourself, personally!"

She sounded perplexed. "A person should answer correctly." She pushed the bedclothes back, and he heard her dressing in the darkness.

"Turn on the light," he suggested.

"Not on your life."

He said, "You're an odd one."

"So are you!" she said, her voice muffled by her dress. He listened to her lace her sneakers, button herself up, then he heard the lock turn on the door.

"This has been," she said poignantly, "a shattering experience."

7

AARON SAT HUNCHED behind a protective row of easels, working on his painting, hidden from the eyes of his instructor, a tall man named Fellows who wandered through and grunted unhappily at the work in progress.

He leaned between the easels and, reaching out his cane, tapped Aaron on the shoulders.

"Ah, Franklin," he scolded. "Behind the barricades!"

"It's not ready for viewing."

"Come out, wherever you are."

"Tomorrow."

Fellows patted his moustache. "My dear chap. Let's have a look."

"Not a chance."

Fellows persisted. "Franklin, you've been in my class for weeks, and I've never seen a thing you've done. What shall I think? Are you actually painting?" He turned and included the class with a wave of his cane. "Perhaps you're performing unnatural acts."

They laughed. Aaron's scowl dissolved. With a flourish,

he removed his canvas and handed it between the easels to the teacher. Fellows grunted, studied, and squinted.

He said nothing. Holding the picture at arm's length, he cocked his head and nodded reflectively as all activity in the room stopped. The only sound was the creaking of the floor as he shifted weight from one polished shoe to the other.

"Ah," he said finally. "Well, well, well." He spoke slowly, pausing theatrically between breaths to touch his ear. "My friends, I have a surprise for you. We are in the presence of a budding talent." He smiled. He returned the picture to Aaron, who quickly shoved it behind his easel.

"How does it feel," he asked, "to be so singled out."

"Maybe you're mistaken."

Fellows' voice boomed out, "My dear boy! You're probably right! Stop by my office after class." He thumped his cane on the floor and signaled the students to work hard. "Press on. Time is money." He winked conspiratorially and marched out.

Joe Carmine, a Brazilian exchange student, said, "He's an old fool."

"Do you know him?"

"Who? Fellows?"

"Yes."

"I know him," Joe said positively. "He don't care."

Fellows returned and snatched the canvas from Aaron.

"Franklin, I'm taking this canvas to my office."

"It's not finished."

Fellows disagreed. "That's the trouble; it's too finished. Abandon it, dear boy. Chuck it aside. Onward and upward."

"I'd like it back."

"Start another."

"I'd like to speak with you privately."

"You would?"

"In your office. Did you really like my picture?"
"Franklin. I'm willing to talk."

"Sit down." Fellows indicated a straight-backed wooden bench in his office. He went behind the desk and slumped into a padded leather club chair. He leaned forward, pressing his fingertips together, and said pleasantly, "Have you ever considered psychiatry?"
"Of course."
"I see."
"What about my picture? You think I've got it?"
"No offense, but you're very neurotic. I once was. I recognize the symptoms. What difference does it make? You don't care what I think."
"I do!"
"No. You think I'm a silly fashion plate, out of date. I know what you think. For what it's worth, I believe you're talented. You're a very young chap with the burden of talent. You're scared. I had it once. A quite big talent. It got to be a burden. Care for a drink?" He pulled open a drawer and brought out a half-empty bottle of Hine cognac.
"Am I really good?"
"Yes, you really are, my dear fellow, and what do you propose to do about it?"
"I'll drink to that."
Fellows crossed his long elegant feet on the top of the desk. Cupping the back of his head in his hands, he tilted his chair and solemnly regarded the ceiling. "Yes. In a moment. We'll both drink to that. However, there's something I must tell you. There's more to it than talent."
"I work hard."
"So does a horse."
Aaron said suspiciously, "Everyone is neurotic."

"Perhaps. There is something maniacal in your painting. I daresay you paint the same picture many times."

"What's wrong with that?"

Fellows consulted a thin gold watch that he removed from his vest pocket. "I would suggest an analyst. I know of some excellent ones."

"What about my picture? Are you sure it's good?"

Fellows wrote a name on a piece of paper, folded it, and handed it to Aaron. "Here's his name and address."

"I don't know what you're talking about, Mr. Fellows, but I'll tell you this. I don't need psychiatry. All I need is instruction in painting."

Fellows poured drinks in two dusty glasses. He handed one to Aaron.

"In fact I don't know anybody alive today who paints better than I do," Aaron said. "Not at my age." He gulped his drink. "What do you think of that!"

Fellows touched the drink to his lips and replaced the glass on the desk. "I quite agree," he said pleasantly, "which is why I am taking the trouble."

"Listen. Are you serious?"

"Your only hope, old boy. Else you'll flounder. I know. It happened to me. I was once damned good, and being good, it scared me. I became a profligate, a drinker and a wastrel. If I had been mediocre merely, the problem wouldn't have come up. Success, or even the chance of success, that's the rub! Failure is no trouble at all. We all embrace failure. It's familiar and grand. But triumph?" He winked. "Watch out for triumph." He drank his brandy. "I had two wives, you know. Not at the same time. They couldn't stand the pace, poor things. Being a failure is a full-time, twenty-four-hour kind of thing, and they died before their time. Not I! I was safe. So long as he fails, man is safe from death." He poured a larger drink and recapped the bottle without offering any to Aaron. "We made friends all over Europe. We even had children. Yet, I wonder sometimes: Whatever became of the paintings?"

"I have forty-three paintings."

"Quantity, old boy. Anyone with half an eye can paint. Widows. Generals. . . ."

"I'm almost seventy years old. I'm older than you. I'm smarter and richer and better educated. Do as you please." He picked up Aaron's painting and handed it to him. "Don't forget this." He indicated the piece of paper.

"I respect your reputation and all that, but I can't see a psychiatrist. My father would have a stroke."

"Don't tell him. Just go. Before it's too late."

"These things cost money!"

"Without it you're doomed."

"I have no money of my own."

Fellows daubed his forehead with the back of his hand. "I'm very tired, Franklin. Go back to the classroom."

"So you see, it's out of the question."

"Shut the door behind you."

Leaving the building, Aaron noticed a large girl in a white raincoat approach him slowly. Leaning forward, she touched him on the sleeve.

"Hello," he said stiffly. "You're the maid. I wondered what happened to you. Someone else is cleaning my room."

She shifted her feet and stood awkwardly, her arms hanging loosely at her sides. "People aren't always maids. They do other things. I've come into some money."

"Good."

She said solemnly, "You're a painter, aren't you?"

"How did you know?"

"People know things."

"What's that mean?"

She lowered her eyes and spoke mysteriously. "I shall inform your father."

He regarded her cautiously. "Why?"

She stared hopelessly.

"Look," he complained, "I have an appointment." He patted her arm and forced a smile. "Good luck to you."

"Don't patronize."

"I have to go."

"Perhaps you should stay."

"I don't know what you want, but I have to get going."

"Hah!"

"What do you want?"

"I intend to tell your parents."

"Tell them what?"

"About us."

"What about us?"

"Well, it's terribly difficult to say. In public." She lowered her voice to a whisper. "You're a father."

"Get away. I mean it."

She said darkly, "You have no right to bully people." She shook her finger at him. "Consider that a warning." She straightened her raincoat and, after gazing mournfully at him, stepped to the side, her head held high.

8

SOL GREETED EACH NEW ARRIVAL acquisitively. He owned the house, the driveway, and the twenty acres of Long Island; the whiskey, the food, the servants were his.

Manny Herzog alighted from his Cadillac and embraced his friend. They beamed at each other.

"Sollie, you son of a gun!"

Ben Katz braked his Jaguar and joined them.

He embraced them in a delighted huddle. Other cars arrived. Sol shook hands and mopped his face and snapped his fingers at circling waitresses.

"Another round!"

Disengaging himself from one group, he rushed to greet Charley Rand.

Moe Fenster brought his wife, a plump lady in a summer mink. Moe grabbed Sol in a headlock; the two fat men tugged each other.

The autumn sun filtered through the foliage and ivy and weeping willows, producing a latticework of tiny bright spots on the parked cars. The heat caused the men to remove their jackets. Ladies fanned themselves with paper plates. Sol darted about, a drink in his hand, a cigar gripped between his pink lips, ordering servants, demanding ice, greeting friends, and slapping backsides.

He and Alma took them inside for a sit-down luncheon. Four leaves had been added to the dining room table. From one end to the other, platters and tureens and bowls of summer food were on display: lobsters, chickens, salamis, crab, shrimps, and molds of salad; melons filled with grapes and berries, tomatoes stuffed with tuna fish; salmon, smoked or fresh. In front of each guest was ten dollars' worth of gray Beluga caviar. Bowls of cream cheese and sour cream dotted the Irish lace table cloth. Crystal glasses, Queen Anne silver, and pewter mugs completed the decor. On the sideboard, enormous silver buckets were filled with soda water: celery tonic, cokes, cherry, raspberry, ginger ale, and Seven Up. Other buckets held beer, German white wines, and Poland water. A corner cupboard showed stacks of freshly baked pies, strudel, tarts, cheese cakes, Napoleons, and eclairs. In front, in a square silver bread box, were stacks of rye breads, chohlas, seeded rolls, bagels, bialis, and, for some of the Protestant wives, two loaves of white.

Sol shouted, getting unsteadily to his feet and raising his Scotch and soda over his head: "To the Porter Street gang! To Boston! To the entire world!"

He sat down heavily, grinning at the cheers his speech provoked. Alma, from the opposite end of the table watched the festivities, the energetic eating, laughing, and sudden bursts of sentimentality as men kissed each other. She sat quietly, her face wearing an expression of forced gaiety, surprised that she could endure so much without complaint.

Sol was speaking. She straightened her back, fixed a smile on her drawn face, and joined him.

"Are you ready?" he asked, his flushed face alive, his plump body tensed with anticipation. "C'mon then."

Moe Fenster, Al Kaplan, and Charley Rand handed their coffee cups to their wives and solemnly walked to the center of the porch where Sol, with a flourish of his arms, announced the first song.

"'Girl of My Dreams,' in honor of the ladies!"

Charley began in a true, clear tenor.

"Girl of my dreams, I love you. Honest I do . . ."

And the others then joined in with: "You are so sweet" in perfect harmony, the notes swelling, dying, and rising again as the bass rolled up from a fifth below the melody, and Sol hung a note a third above and retained it. The baritone moved over the melody, below it, and found his note, and, as they reached "Sweet," the room filled with the clear, loud chord. They held it and inundated themselves with it, arms about each other, their faces hot and cheerful, so proud of each other, so sentimental, that they ended in an abrupt, embarrassed rush.

When the applause ceased, they sang again. All the old songs: "Take Me Back to Old New York," "The Fall River Line," "Second Hand Rose," "Rose of Picardy," "Rose of Washington Square," "New Coon in Town," "The Shade of the Old Apple Tree," "Gee, But I Hate To Go Home Alone," "I'm Afraid To Go Home in the Dark," "Hello Central, Give Me No Man's Land," "The Rose of No Man's Land." At five o'clock, they stopped.

"Listen," Sol said. "How about a race?"

Jumping in place, beating his arms as if they were cold, Sol clenched his teeth and waited for the start. The others shared his nervousness. They edged ahead of the mark and inched back—the five melancholy men, quietly concentrating on the long track, eyeing each other for signs of weakness. Fenster crouched professionally, his white shoes rimmed with dust, his gabardine knee touching the grass. Cohen removed his wristwatch, fountain pen, glasses, and wallet. He placed them in a neat pile to one side. He spit on his pale hands, rubbed them together, and copied Fenster's crouch. Herzog stood upright, leaning forward, his cuffs rolled, his shirt open at the throat. Lefcourt worked his mouth and smoothed his thin hair and breathed deeply.

"On your mark!" Minnie Marcus cleared her throat and got them started. "Get set. Go!"

Digging furiously, his knees pumping, Sol took the lead. Head up, shoulders back, his stomach partially sucked in, he led for the first ten yards while Herzog, whose long stride seemed effortless, reached him and began to pass. Sol fought off the challenge for a few feet, then gritted his teeth and redoubled his effort as Herzog slowly pulled ahead. To his right, he heard the heavy breathing of Fenster, running awkwardly, elbows and knees flying wildly. He too reached Sol and remained at his side while Herzog held the lead.

Someone fell behind them. They heard a loud thump and a groan. Fenster gasped from the side of his mouth.

"It's Lefcourt. He tripped. Cohen, too."

Sol grimaced and strained and fought off Fenster's challenge. Slowly, he drew ahead. The others were behind him. His problem was Herzog, who seemed unreachable. With each long stride, he gained ground. Sol cursed the long, elegant back, the rolled pants, the graceful attitude. He lowered his head in determined pursuit. At the first turn by the apple orchard, Herzog looked back, smiling. Sol stared at him. He saw no fatigue on the leader's face. Herzog was tireless. So he pumped his arms and forced more speed from his fat body. His chest hurt and he cursed the cigars he smoked, and the food and drinks, and urged himself forward. At the second turn, he had closed the gap and no more than fifteen yards separated them. Sol's head throbbed; his mouth was dry; his eyes burned. Only fifteen yards.

They were nearing the final turn at the oak tree. He could hear the cheering and laughter at the finish line. But he wasn't fooling. Desire to catch Herzog so obsessed him, he lunged and lurched. He cautioned himself.

"Don't break stride. Keep after him, the bastard."

Herzog was definitely out of wind. His head hung, his shoulders drooped. Sol glared fiercely and propelled his exhausted body forward, like some wild animal plunging through thickets. Herzog faltered. His legs parodied his earlier grace. His shirttail flopped out of his pants. His back was dark with perspiration. In a few seconds Sol would catch him. He was sure of it. Suddenly, he heard a hoarse gasping. A strangled cry. Someone called his name.

"I've got you, Sollie."

My God! he thought. Cohen! Another one. Fury with Cohen and Herzog pushed him forward. His legs were numb, his arms and neck ached. Each step was a torture. But he had it won. Herzog dropped limply to one side. He would never finish. He sat on the grass and grinned stupidly as Sol thundered past with Cohen inches behind.

Alma's shriek surprised him. He heard her voice just before he pitched forward, his open mouth against the dirt and pebbles.

9

WHEN HE AWAKENED, the guests were gone. The house was quiet. He found himself in his silk pajamas. A mild October wind blew outside his room. He wet his lips and closed his eyes. A coronary was his diagnosis. The heat didn't help. Once he could have breezed past them. No more races. A strict diet. Cut out the smoking.

It was a heart attack. He was lucky. One more and he was a goner.

He opened one eye. He had wanted to say something cheerful, a joke, like, "I ain't dead." Was he paralyzed? Had he suffered a stroke? He worked his fingers. He lifted his chin. He forced himself to breathe calmly. He worked his jaw tentatively, opening it and closing it. He blinked his eyes. He twitched his nose and furrowed his forehead. He tried a second time. A croak emerged.

Alma was at his side.

"Thank God! He's speaking." She gripped his hand in her dry fingers and gazed feverishly at him.

Doctor Atlee took his pulse and examined his eyes. "You'll live."

"Oh, Sol!" Alma collapsed on the bed and hugged him. Too weak to respond, he said, "Shhh."

Herzog spoke sheepishly.

"Glad you made it, Sollie. Stupidity, racing at our age." Sol thought: I beat him.

"Don't worry," Alma cautioned. "I've sent for Aaron."

Someone was running towards his room.

Aaron charged into his parents' darkened bedroom, his hair falling over his forehead.

"Where is he?" he demanded. "How is he feeling?"

He ran to the window and opened the venetian blind with a fierce tug. Moonlight illuminated the room. He raised the window.

"Let some air in here. A little light! This man is as good as he ever was. Put on some music. I know him! He understands noise!"

"Go away. Back off from him. Can't you understand? He's lost his voice. He fell while running."

Sol, partially sitting, propped by pillows, wished to complain.

"He's trying to speak." Alma tugged at Aaron's sweater. He withdrew from her grasp and stood at attention, his neck stretching.

"Then why is he silent? Is this a game?"

The doctor cleared his throat professionally. "These things happen. Loss of speech is not uncommon."

"This is no crisis!"

Alma demanded he keep his voice down.

"No! He may be too old to run a race, but that man's not dying!"

She gasped. "Nobody said dying!"

"You did! You called me at school. 'A terrible thing!' you said. 'Your father! Come! Come home.' I caught a train. I found a taxi!"

Sol stared. He turned his head with irritation and said clearly, "Cut out the racket!"

"He talked. What about that!"

The doctor said, "A good sign."

Alma smoothed her husband's hair. "My prayers are answered."

Sol closed his eyes. Color returned in unhealthy splotches. His breath grew deeper. His fists unclenched and his mouth opened. They heard the familiar sounds of his thunderous snoring.

10

ELSA MOST OWNED AN ART GALLERY on Fifty-seventh Street. She was at least one hundred pounds overweight and any effort quickly exhausted her limited endurance. Certain twilight men adored her.

When Aaron was announced by her receptionist, she greeted him herself.

Her size surprised him. First came her breasts, followed by her beach-ball stomach and, finally, like two hockey pucks, her tiny feet carrying the rest of her into view.

"Hi," she said.

He showed her one of the pictures. She peered momentarily. "As Dawson said, I have risen to the morning danger and feel proud."

"Do you like it?" he asked.

"I simply love it," she said. "I'll give you two hundred dollars for both pictures."

"Hold on," he said. "How did you hear of me? Why did you write to me?"

"It doesn't matter how, you're here now, aren't you?"

She collapsed into a Miller chair. When she finished seating herself, she waved her flipper hand.

"That's it. Done and done. My information was correct. You're talented."

"No you don't," he said, clutching his two pictures. "You don't even know about me."

Her chuckle frightened him.

"I know your name. It's Aaron Franklin. It was kind of you to come in from school."

He backed away towards the door. "I thought these things took time."

"Ho!" she said in her basso voice. "If you mean it's irregular, I quite agree. Helga Fern called. She instructed me to buy two pictures. It's as simple as that."

"Who is Helga Fern?"

"I thought you knew her. She certainly knows you."

"I never heard of her."

"She is Corliss and Vernon's daughter. I would say she's extremely rich." She shifted her bulk and closed her eyes. "I'm tired," she complained. "Is it a deal or isn't it a deal?"

He tightened his grip. "I need time to think. I never meant to actually sell them. I wanted an opinion. From an expert."

"I have given you an opinion."

"I don't know. Maybe you're no expert."

"You're making me sleepy, young man. I've offered you good money for your pictures. By the way, let me see them."

"They're nudes."

"I have a purchaser. She believes in you. Let's face it, for two hundred dollars, I'd sell crap on a stick, if you catch my meaning."

"I don't sell to total strangers."

"I'm not sure I approve."

"That's all right."

"Wait," she said. "No hard feelings."

"None."

"Do us a favor, will you, ducks?" She waved to him. "Help us out of the chair. I should never have sat down."

He called the receptionist, who shook her head.

"Sorry, sir. I hurt myself earlier this month. She wouldn't have sat down if you weren't there to help." She smiled apologetically.

"I'm sorry too." He opened the door. "I have to see my father. He's been sick."

"Come back here," she called. "Do us a favor."

Helga entered, hitting him with the door, her short blond hair plastered to her forehead with water. Her white raincoat was streaked with grease, as were her hands.

"No one helps people when they have to change tires." She leaned against the door.

From the chair, Elsa demanded her name. "You can't barge in here. Only by appointment." She pleaded with Aaron. "Give us a hand, ducks."

He said, "It's you! You followed me!"

"The man in the rental office said the tires were sound. People shouldn't lie."

"You rented a car to follow me!"

"Yes. They will expel me from college with poor attendance records. But you don't care."

"Get out of my life!"

"Not so fast," Elsa said. "Perhaps you and your girl friend could get me out of here."

Helga cried, "Nobody cares." She leaned over Elsa and asked about the paintings. "Did you buy them for me? I'm Corliss Fern's daughter. I called."

Aaron hugged his pictures. "So you're the one."

"The offer was for five hundred dollars."
"She's not my girl friend."
Helga moaned. "They will expel me. All because of you."
"Come on, sweetie. Help us out of the chair."

11

"ACH." MAX BREST INSPECTED HIS WRISTWATCH: he had overslept. He heaved his plump body about in the bedclothes and rubbed his eyes.

He stood squarely in the center of his room, his white hairless calves, like two stanchions, bracing his nightshirted figure. His wife snored gently in the twin bed.

He yanked on the table light. He extracted a cigar from his humidor. He lit it with an ornate table lighter, and proceeded to dress himself. He entered his bathroom and relieved himself with impatient force. He swallowed a handful of antacid pills, washed them down with tap water, and reinserted his cigar, which he held clamped between his front teeth as he lathered and shaved his fat chins with a heavy old-fashioned Gillette razor. The steam and smoke obscured the mirror, but he knew so well the geography of his cheeks—the dew-laps, the tender underbelly of the second chin—that he rapidly scraped his gray whiskers, washed out the razor, and patted talcum under his plump white arms.

At seven-ten, his front doorbell rang. His first patient arrived every morning at eight-thirty, prompt but never early. He called to his wife: "Bella, some tradesman. Deal with him. I have shortly a patient."

In her flannel robe and felt slippers, Bella moved across the large living room, shuffling her feet against the Persian throw rugs.

She tugged at the heavy front door.

"Yes?" She squinted into the bright morning light. "What is it?" She stepped aside, and looking past him down the steps, refocused and raised her head.

He saluted with two fingers to his eyebrow and flicked his fingertips in her direction. He said nothing. His smile radiated good cheer. She marveled at his face, the blue of his eyes.

Her smile equaled his. "What do you wish?"

"Is there a doctor in this house?"

"I beg your pardon?"

"Does Max Brest live here?" He leaned towards her and spoke softly. "I must see him, huh?"

"Do you have an appointment?"

"My name is Aaron Franklin. A student of Archie Fellows."

"I see."

"Don't you believe me?"

"I'm sure you are if you say you are."

"Thank you."

"One moment, please." She backed up, half closing the door behind her. "Moment, please. I get him."

Aaron inserted his foot inside the door.

"No tricks," he informed her. "I've come a long way."

Brest arrived, nodding and beaming expectantly. He whispered rapidly to Bella. "Yes. Yes. What is it?"

"Max! His foot! In the door!"

09

"Yes. Yes. I'm not blind. I see a foot."

"A giant. He wants to see you."

"Ah." He moved his wife behind him and partially opened the door. "Yes?" He gazed benignly up at Aaron.

"Are you Dr. Brest?"

"Yah!"

Holding his foot in place, Aaron took a deep breath. He said slowly, with great feeling, "I am here to see you. Mr. Fellows recommended you. I'll do what I can to improve."

"Why are you willing to do these marvelous things?"

"I'm serious."

"I'm sure you are, but I am very busy. I have no time at present. Call for an appointment."

"Don't you have visiting hours?"

"One doesn't just arrive for an appointment. I am not a veterinarian."

"I want to see you, now. Apparently I need help!"

"I must insist. Phone for an appointment!" Brest shot the door forward in an attempt to dislodge Aaron's foot. The suddenness of the move succeeded. He leaned with all his strength and almost closed it, but Aaron, who had been slightly off balance, recovered in time to keep the door from catching in its lock. He shoved with both his arms. Inside, Bella joined her husband in his struggle with the door. Their combined push held off his countercharge. The door seesawed momentarily until Aaron's strength overcame the two old people. The door swung open.

"You're crazy. I call the police."

"Are you hurt?"

"I see no one without an appointment. Not even ruffians."

Aaron touched his forehead. During the banging and shoving, he had cut it.

"He's bleeding," Bella said.

"No, I'm not," Brest said.

"Not you. Him. Look at his head."

Aaron said dramatically, "It's nothing. A war wound."

"What war?" she cried. "Get him inside."

Brest stepped closer. "It's a simple abrasion. Nothing serious."

Aaron insisted. "How about an hour of your time?"

"You are a persistent fellow. However, there are laws in this country. You are guilty of breaking and entering. I can easily call the police and have you arrested. This will end your little recital."

Aaron said, "I'm a friend of Mr. Fellows."

Brest opened his mouth to protest, then he leaned his head back and smiled, which eased the tension in the vestibule. Bella smiled.

"You come back another day."

"No. I must see you now."

Brest snapped his fingers. "Bella. Call the police!"

The two men heard her shuffle across the living room, lift the phone, and say clearly, "I want please, the police. An emergency."

Brest said triumphantly, "Your arrogance has disappeared."

"I thought you were supposed to help people."

"That is correct! By appointment only."

"No hard feelings."

"None!"

"Don't you intend shaking hands?"

"I'm an analyst, not a diplomat. Call me later in the day. Possibly I have a cancellation."

"How much do you get an hour?"

"We discuss that later."

"Call off the police. My father is recovering from a heart attack."

Brest dismissed the idea with a wave of his palm. "Don't worry. I'm sure she made no call." He grinned. "We too are allowed our dramatics." Brest watched him descend the steps. He entered and closed the door behind him. "Bella. Did you actually call?"

"Of course not."

"What did you think?"

"He's a beautiful young fellow. So straight up and down."

"Yah. A maniac too."

"You think so?"

"Well, not a maniac. But nutty, I think. We see. He might be an interesting fellow."

The doorbell rang again. Brest jerked it open and said with heat, "Get going!"

"You don't understand. There's a pregnant woman following me. A giant!"

Brest reconsidered. "That's very interesting."

"Wherever I go, there she is!"

"I see. There she is!" He opened the door and stepped aside. "I give you a half hour. That's all."

"You won't regret it."

Aaron followed him inside. He lay back on a leather couch and placed his head on a paper napkin.

"Well? Why are you so silent for?" Brest puffed his cigar. "Are you thinking of that giant?"

"I was considering the spot on your ceiling."

Brest crossed his legs and sat on his feet. "Stop wasting time, please. You were speaking about a pregnant giant."

"I know."

"Come now. Begin."

"Why should I talk to you?"

"The question is: Why did you come here?"
"I have no idea."
Brest laughed. "So! Didn't you consider it a bit strange? This pregnant giant?"
"Yes."
"Then why don't you talk?"
"I don't know."
The telephone at Brest's elbow rang. He answered it brusquely.
"Yah?" He listened, puffing nervously at his cigar. He stared incredulously at the phone. Then he laughed. "I don't run a dating bureau." He grinned. "A call for you. From a Miss Helga Fern."
"That's the one!"
"She says she's waiting for you! Did you make her pregnant, or does she simply imagine she is pregnant?"
"It's her word against mine."
"This is not a law court. Did you make her pregnant?"
"What do you think?"
"I rely on you for a first-hand report."
Aaron was silent.
"Are you the father?"
"I can't understand you."
"The question is simple."
"It's your accent. You have a heavy accent."
"Answer, please, my question."
"How long have you been in America?"
"Over twenty years."
"That's long enough to lose an accent."
"If you are the father, we should discuss it. If you are not, we simply tell the young lady to go away."
"She won't go away. She's after me."
"You are an annoying fellow. We have established the

fact that she follows you. The question is: Are you guilty?"

"What part of Germany did you come from?"

"Not Germany. Vienna. We are getting nowhere."

"Well, it's difficult to talk about it."

"Stop being foolish. Remember, you crashed in here, whining about your life. 'Help me,' you said. Nu? How can I help you when all the time you discuss my heritage. How many girls do you know? Is Helga the only one?"

"I'm very much in love with a girl. Polly Gang. Her mother is dying. In a way, it's her fault. After she left I went back to my room and there she was."

"Helga!"

"Right. Helga was there. I was in no position to protect myself."

Brest laughed so hard he began to cough.

"I'm serious. I met her and she dashed off with her father."

"A touching story. Where is Polly now?"

"She said she'd call. She never called."

"Did you call her?"

"It was her turn."

"She may need your support. Especially with a dying mother."

"You're right."

"So. Now we return to the giant, Helga. The one who carries your unborn child."

"Yeah."

"It could be worse."

"How do you know?"

"Actually, I don't. But I say it sometimes."

"You're all right."

"You said that before. You keep on speaking about me, but you are the one who needs help."

"Does that mean you don't?"

Brest relit the cigar and spoke impatiently. "Look. I am a busy man. If you want to waste time, go somewhere else."

"Suppose I am the father. What do I do?"

"Marry her."

"Can't she get rid of it? I don't want it."

"Abortion is against the law."

"She's too tall. And her hair is too short."

"You should have thought of that when you opened your fly."

"You sound like my father."

"Don't you like your father?"

"As I said before, it's difficult understanding you."

Brest looked at his wristwatch. "We stop now. Call me next week. We continue then."

"Are you throwing me out?"

Brest walked to the door and opened it. "Goodbye, Mr. Franklin."

Aaron stood and looked down at him. "How much do I owe you?"

"We talk next week." He held out his soft hand.

Aaron walked down the steps. He found a drugstore and called Polly's number.

"It's me. Aaron."

"Hi. How's school!?"

"How's your mother?"

He heard her sob. "It was awful. She died yesterday. Poor Daddy. You should see him. He fell apart and started drinking again."

"I'm sorry about your mother."

She was crying. "I didn't realize how much I loved her. You don't know how much you love them until they die."

"I'll come right over."

"Are you in New York?"

"Yes. I had some personal business."

"Listen. Don't come here. Meet me at the Beverly Funeral Home."

As he was leaving the booth, a large girl darted out of the store.

12

THE TAXI STOPPED before the funeral home. He saw Helga near the building, her eyes shielded against the morning sun, her raincoat collar like a cowl around her chin.

"It's you, Helga Fern! You're ruining me. You've sent me to a psychiatrist."

She said darkly, "How about unwed mothers? Their lives are ruined."

"What are you doing here? How do you know so much about me?"

"People have ways." She slouched against the building. "I followed you to college. I saw it all. It's necessary to follow you. You're the father of my unborn child."

Tears formed in her pale eyes. She blew her nose. "The doctor who examined me hurt me more than was absolutely necessary. He moved his hands in a social manner rather than a scientific one and remained in the room while I dressed myself."

"There are tests."

"I have morning sickness, dizziness, and a general sense

of malaise. Also, I urinated in a bottle. The next day I was so violently sick, I coughed blood. I humped over the toilet bowl and gagged and vomited and gripped my head. I watched the water beneath me turn such an angry red, I believed I would die before morning. Don't ask me if I'm pregnant. The fact is: I am pregnant. What do you intend to do about it?"

"I don't know!"

She flinched and raised her arms for protection.

"Now listen. Go away. I'll call you tomorrow."

"Oh, sure. That's a good one."

He rushed past her, through the door of the funeral home, searching for Polly.

Gus Gang was completing the funeral arrangement. An organ would play Vivaldi (Clara loved Vivaldi as she did all music). The casket would remain closed.

He wore a clean blue suit and had shaved for the first time in a week.

Polly said, "How is it going?"

"Just fine. The funeral will be tomorrow at two, and I think that Clara would like it."

"Poor Mother. It's hard to believe she's finally dead."

"I'm alive," he said bitterly.

She held his hand. "I'm glad."

He looked up in pain. "Oh God. Like a bad penny."

Aaron advanced, head down, hands jammed in his pockets.

"I'm not up to that," Gus complained. "I'll see you later."

Aaron said, "I'm sorry about your mother. I've missed you."

"You have?"

He hugged her. "I'm going to protect you. I'm a patriot in your country."

"Talk nicely."

"I have definite troubles of my own."

"Like what?"

"Look!" he blurted. "I hate to burden you."

"What is it?"

"There's this girl," he said slowly, his voice a confidential whisper.

"What girl?"

"A Helga Fern. Claims I made her pregnant."

"Are you sure?"

"Wherever I go, she's there. Like an allegory."

She patted his arm. "Come on. No tricks. I have to get back to Daddy."

"What tricks. This is serious. This is a bad time for me. A time of fearful expectation."

"What does she want?"

"Me."

"Well, why does she, if you don't want her?"

"I don't know."

"There's got to be a reason."

He explained.

"What a terrible thing!" Polly whistled.

"You mean my getting her pregnant?"

She smacked her fist against the palm of her hand. She stared at the floor. "It's a rotten thing," she said bitterly.

"Well," he said uneasily. "I told you. I thought she was a maid."

"A lowdown shame!"

"She even looked like a maid."

"Something must be done. You're right about that!"

"She still looks like a maid!"

"I'm not angry with you. After all, you're just a boy. Boys don't stand a chance with girls. Boys are just visitors. Let's go out and talk to her. We'll give her the name of an abortionist."

He said quickly, "I'll take care of it. I don't need your help."

"If you're my friend, you'll let me talk to her."

"Don't take charge."

"You asked me to help. I intend helping!"

13

NOBODY BOTHERED TOBY FERN; his size provoked respect. His pink skin and perfect teeth indicated a robustness seldom seen outside the wide screen of a technicolor movie.

He finished his fiftieth push-up and squinted in the morning sun.

Breathing heavily, he commenced a series of sit-ups, stopping at one hundred and toweling himself and shouting in the empty room.

Upstairs, the front doorbell rang.

He draped two towels over his head and put on an extra sweatshirt. Drafts were a threat in his overheated condition. Wearing a robe, he walked upstairs and through a real hall that led out to the front parlor. He crossed the room barefoot and, going through the vestibule, reached the heavy front door and opened it. A pretty girl stood there.

"Can I help you?"

"Are you an Arab?" She smiled up at him. "Does a Helga live here?"

"I can't stand in the open doorway."

"Are you her brother?"

"I'm in a draft."

"I was wondering. Would you ask her to come to the door?"

"She's not home."

"Where is she?"

"At college," he said impatiently. "What's your name?"

"Polly Gang. I want to discuss some things with her."

"I have to take a shower. I'm sorry."

She looked past him at the sparkling chandelier, the cream-colored carpeting, the satin drapes, the bowls of cut flowers in formal displays, the curve of steps that spiraled up at the far end of the hallway.

"Beautiful," she said.

He shifted his weight and fingered his robe.

"It must be lovely living in so nice a home."

"Very comfortable. Are you a friend of Helga's?"

"Comfortable?" She smiled shyly. "It's so much more than that. It's really quite stunning."

"All the furniture is registered. It's all authentic, actually. By that I mean each piece is authenticated as to date and designer by a dealer in London."

"I'm sure it is."

"Look here," he said after an awkward moment. "Why don't you come in? I can't stay in this cold air."

"Not if your sister isn't here. I'll be back another time."

"Don't go."

He surprised her. "I must. I came to see Helga."

"There's no rush."

"No rush? What do you mean?"

"I didn't intend it to sound that way. You surprised me. I opened the door, and there you were, standing there. You're very beautiful, you know."

"Thank you."

"Helga will be home soon. She often drops in in the afternoon."

"There's no need to put yourself out. I'll come by again. I should have called first."

"Ping-Pong. Do you happen to play?"

"Did you say Ping-Pong?"

"Yes!"

"Are you sure you have a sister named Helga?"

"Ask anyone."

"The Ping-Pong's O.K."

"I'm very glad."

She walked past him and surveyed the hallway a second time.

"The table's downstairs. In the gym."

"Do you live here alone? You and your sister?"

"Oh, no," he said, holding open the door for her and indicating a stairway. "My parents live here. It's their place. I'm just waiting until I can afford a place of my own."

Polly walked down the stairs. "If I had a place like this, I'd never leave. It's marvelous. Oh, look!" she exclaimed at the bottom of the steps. "An entire gymnasium!"

The large room contained parallel bars, weights, pulley, mats, a boxing ring, punching bags, heavy bags, an exercise bicycle, a rowing machine, chinning bars and a collection of large leather balls, a Ping-Pong table, a billiard table, and a small swimming pool.

"Only a practice pool," Toby explained. "Only fifty feet. Good to practice turns."

Taking up a paddle and a ball, she said, "I'm ready."

"So am I."

"Let's start."

Before he could set himself, she snapped a fast serve

across the net. It bounced on his side and shot past his arm.

"Say!" he exclaimed, retrieving the ball from under his bare feet. "You're good. Where did you learn to serve like that?"

"One-love."

He tossed it to her and she caught it expertly, and served again without pausing. The ball hit him in the chest.

"Two for me."

He braced himself. On her third serve, he stepped back and sliced the ball in a cross-court return. She reached forward and cut to his backhand. He moved in for a slam. She blocked it. He banged the weak return down the middle, but she caught the high bouncing smash with a tennis overhead that nicked the edge of the table.

"Three."

She was serving. He chopped it back. She returned deep to his forehand. He slammed it hard, but caught the net.

"Four. Ball, please."

On her fifth serve, Toby undercut his shot which brought her forward, and, when her return was soft, he wound up and hit a forehand smash that moved so fast she didn't see it.

She regarded him grudgingly. "You serve. One to four."

"Most women athletes are lumpy. You're not. You're quite remarkable. I'm surprised you're Helga's friend. Most of her friends are dreadful. She makes friends with the worst girls in her class."

"One-four."

Toby discovered that when he hit a normal serve she stepped back and pummeled the ball from either side: backhand or forehand, and he was compelled to slice the ball instead of simply getting it into play. By the time the score was tied at nine all, she had affected a vicious chop that undercut his shot and caused him to net the ball or, at best, return weakly. At fourteen to fifteen, he was breathing hard and perspiring. He removed his robe and his sweatshirt and stood waiting, his naked chest heaving from exertion. She complimented him.

"You're muscular." He blushed. She whipped a shot past him and said, "Sixteen-fifteen."

"No," he said politely. "Fifteen-fifteen."

"Righto," she said. "Whatever you want."

"It's not what I want. It's what the score is. It's fifteen for you and fifteen for me."

"Ah," she said, slightly puzzled.

"Right," he said, squaring his shoulders.

She tilted her head. "Is it my serve? Or is it yours? I forget."

"It's mine. We changed at twelve-thirteen . . ." As he spoke, she rifled another shot, but he caught the ball in his hand.

"My serve," she said. "The score is sixteen to fourteen."

She sat on the floor. "I'm weary. Got a Coke?"

"You're a fine Ping-Pong player."

"For a girl."

"Of course. You *are* a girl and . . ." he blushed ". . . a fine one. I mean it!" He fought his way back into his sweatshirt.

She wiped her forehead with her handkerchief and sighed. "I need a shower."

"Take one! Here. Use Helga's room."

"You don't even know me."

"Any friend of Helga's."

"What's Helga like? Do you think she's pretty?"

"I thought you knew her."

"I wanted your opinion."

"Well, then, you know!"

"No I don't. Know what?"

85

"About Helga."

"What about her?"

"You know," he said with embarrassment. "Her height. She's six feet tall."

Polly whistled.

"Six feet is hardly a giant!"

"It's quite tall though!"

"You mean you don't actually *know* Helga?"

"Not *actually*. I know *about* her."

"I'm delighted you came. For any reason at all."

"I am too. It was great fun. The game."

"Want to swim? I could practice turns."

She stood and placed her raincoat over her arm. "I have to get back. My father will worry."

"I like you. A lot. How about a swim?"

She heard an angry woman coming from the corridor above. "Who's making that fearful sound?"

A door opened. "Who's down there?"

He apologized. "It's Mother. Something is bothering her."

"What are you doing? Get dressed. We're going to the theater."

"I'm with a friend, Mother."

"The friend must go!"

"But, Mother."

"TOBY!" The voice preceded loud thumping on the stairs. "I'm coming down to get you!"

Polly giggled. "She's kidding!"

He shook his head adamantly.

Corliss appeared, her tweed skirt slapping her calves as she advanced forcefully into the room. "Take a shower and get some clothes on. Your famous father has theater tickets."

"Now wait a second, Mother. This girl happens to be a friend of mine. And a friend of Helga's."

"Helga has no friends!"

The phone rang.

"Let the maid answer it," Toby said.

"I fired them. The lot. This morning. They were stealing silverware!" She picked up the receiver. "Hello."

The voice on the other end had a heavy German accent. "Ya?" he said. "This is Mrs. Corliss Fern?"

"It is!" She covered the phone with her hand. "Some refugee."

"I'm calling to inform you your daughter Helga is at present in my office."

"Your office? What kind of office do you have?"

"It's very nice. Done all in wood panels and with leather."

"What about Helga?"

"Exactly! What about her? She's at present collapsed on my sofa. And I would move her into another room, but she's too large. You see I have many patients. They come one after the other. In order. When one collapses it affects the others. They begin to pile up like a logjam."

"Who are you!"

"I am Dr. Max Brest."

"What kind of doctor?"

"I am a psychoanalyst. I treat people who are neurotic. Your daughter is a neurotic."

"How do you know?"

"It's simple. Only neurotics come to my office."

"Let me speak to her this instant."

"Madam. If you are not here inside of a half hour, I call an ambulance."

"What's wrong with her?"

"Nothing is wrong with her. Except a normal dosage of paranoia, narcissism, and megalomania. Also she is convinced she's pregnant."

14

SOL FRANKLIN LIT A FORBIDDEN CIGAR in the quiet of his paneled office. Starting with nothing, son of immigrant parents, he had quit school and gone to work for an uncle in the dry goods line who paid him a dollar a week. He remained there until he was seventeen and was earning twelve dollars a week as a combination salesman, bookkeeper, and buyer. The firm went bankrupt. It was Mischa's fault. His father Mischa had been unemployed since leaving Russia, twenty years earlier. A placid, kindly man whose only pleasure was eating herring, drinking tea, and interpreting the Talmud, no one wanted to hire him. Finally, the uncle agreed to put him on as a part-time clerk. Mischa repaid this kindness by convincing the other clerks they were being exploited. He pulled them out on strike.

The sight of all his employees on the street with picket signs so infuriated the uncle that he grabbed two of the delivery men along with Mischa and attempted to crush them like fruit. This effort produced a coronary. He died in the street, his great arms flailing at Mischa's placid face.

Sol puffed his cigar and thought of his father. A bad husband, a bad father. He had permitted his wife to take in sewing. It was said that certain traits reappeared every other generation. Perhaps Aaron would be another Mischa. A good-for-nothing.

It was a year of deaths. Mischa, who swam each winter in Boston Harbor, died of a stroke as he emerged from icy water on the coldest day of the year. His wife, who stood shivering on the shore where she guarded his clothing, watched him clutch his thin chest, stumble, and call out soundlessly, his voice drowned by the cries of gulls and the winter wind. Sol worked at the time for a wholesale coal dealer. He was summoned by his wild-eyed mother. He rushed to the door and dragged her in. "What? What?" he shouted, thinking she had lost her mind, seeing her disheveled hair, her unbuttoned coat. "Your poppa," she mumbled. "My Mischa." "What? What?" "He's gone." "Where?" "To heaven!" She shrieked.

Cohen, the coal dealer, appeared from upstairs where he had been eating lunch. "What's going on?" he demanded, his napkin stuck in his collar. "What in hell are we running here?"

"Ah, Cohen," she admonished him, recognizing him from the neighborhood. "Cohen. You came here in steerage with him. And with me. We are all Jews, Cohen."

Sol apologized. "You see, Mr. Cohen. My father died. She's upset. Understandable." He had never heard his mother speak so many words at one time. And in English. Usually his parents communicated by grunts and sighs.

"How did it happen, Mama?"

She merely shook her head and clasped her arms about his waist and moaned, "Oy! My Mischa."

Cohen wiped a bit of whitefish from his chin. "So. Mischa is dead. Believe me, he's better off."

"Why," Sol asked, his voice rising, "do you say such a thing, Mr. Cohen?"

"Life was difficult for him. He never integrated with America. Always a greenhorn. And watch your mouth. You're talking to a boss."

"And you?" she asked, her little eyes red and swollen. "You talk like that to a widow?"

Sol demanded to know where his father was.

"On the beach," she said numbly.

"You left him on the beach? Alone?"

"God, no! With a policeman. He covered him with a blanket." She lapsed into Yiddish; then, as if the effort of so many words had affected her face, she covered it with shaky hands and slumped against Sol's desk where she stamped her feet and cursed at God.

"Get her out of here!" Cohen said. "What will the clientele think?"

Sol stood between them, breathing hard, looking fiercely, first at Cohen, then at his mother. He felt dizzy and confused. He whirled and spoke to his employer.

"If you say one more word to my mother, I'll punch you."

Cohen, a stocky man in his forties, prided himself on his flat stomach. "Tell your son he's fired!"

Then Sol hit him. The blow broke Cohen's nose. Blood spurted over his chin down his napkin and onto his vest, his pants, and his high-buttoned patent-leather shoes.

Cohen fell to the ground holding his nose.

"Oy!" she cried, looking down at him. "You've killed Cohen. Two deaths."

Cohen screamed, "Police! Murderer!" His three small children ran down the stairs and saw their father. They began weeping. Mrs. Cohen, a skinny woman, appeared. "Morris," she moaned, "who did this thing?"

"I did. He insulted me."

"Get out, you pig." She rushed to her wounded husband. He spoke weakly. "Sarah. Get the police!"

"How about widows?" Sol's mother demanded, sobbing still, but ready to protect her firstborn.

"What?" Mrs. Cohen noticed her for the first time. "Bessie Franklin. What are you doing here?"

"I'm a widow, Fannie. Mischa just died."

"Oh, my God!" Fannie, who had attended Needle and Trade School with Sol's mother, ran to her and embraced her. The two women rocked and sobbed together while Sol grudgingly helped Cohen to his feet.

He held the bloody napkin against his upper lip and stopped the flow of blood. He helped Cohen into a chair.

"Goodbye, Cohen. I'm quitting as of today." He waved to the oldest child. "Get some wet towels and clean up your father."

Sitting in his big leather chair, by the window that overlooked Bryant Park, Sol found himself smiling. He stamped his cigar out in a silver ashtray that bore the inscription: "To Mr. Solomon Franklin, a fine boss, from his employees, on the twenty-fifth anniversary of the founding of the Beauty Bud Undergarment and Nightgown Company, 1962. Mazel for the next fifty years."

The buzzer sounded. It was his secretary.

He grunted. "Where's my son? Have you seen him around?"

"No, sir," she said. "I'm sorry."

"When you see him, tell him he's late and have him come in."

"Even if the meeting is going on?"

"Of course! He's my son!"

"Hello, Pop. How are you feeling?"

He looked up. His son stood before his desk, tense and pale in a turtleneck sweater and corduroy pants.

"That's some way to dress. This is a place of business."

"I didn't come to be yelled at."

"I'm pointing out how you look. It's out of my hands entirely."

"I wanted to see you. Something terrible has happened."

"I can see that. Sit down."

"I haven't time to sit. I have to talk to you!"

"Don't be a big shot!"

Aaron regarded him quizzically. "Will you listen?"

"I'll listen. But first, you listen! It's a rough life for the learner."

"I may need help."

"I got an important meeting in a minute. Stick around."

"This is vital!"

"Maybe you'll learn something." He pushed a button on his desk. Several men entered the room.

Like a conductor taking tickets, Aaron made the rounds, shaking each man's hand and smiling politely when they joked about his clothes.

This, he realized, was the sales staff. They wore tan Italian suits, dark ties, alligator shoes, and shirts that showed a lot of French cuff and high spread collars. Their nails were polished, their hair was cut short and sleek, and they resembled members of a wealthy Mexican polo team rather than lingerie salesmen.

"We've got the new ads, Sol. The whole spring campaign. Frankly, I think the agency has outdone themselves." One man removed large sheets of paper from a manilla envelope and, like an Arab displaying his wares, spread them on the floor.

After two careful circles, Sol pointed a polished shoe at one of the layouts. "Not bad," he said. "It's O.K. You're all right, Lou. Smart. Watch Lou, Aaron. You could learn a few things."

Lou picked up the layout and placed it on Sol's desk. His salesmen grouped themselves behind him like a singing group. The paper showed a large color photograph of a pretty girl waking up in a sun-filled room. She was stretching and smiling. Beneath the picture was the caption in black type: FOR MORNING GLORY, WAKE UP IN BEAUTY BUD.

"That's the ticket," Sol said. "It looks expensive." He seated himself behind his desk and folded his hands before him like a schoolboy. "It's what the competition is doing but, since they're doing O.K., I see no reason why a copy could be wrong." He shook his head emphatically. "It's hitting the nail on the head!" He looked past the salesmen and glanced at Aaron. "What do you think?" He winked at the men. "He's artistic."

"I don't know," he said uneasily.

"What?" Sol leaned forward. He cupped his ear with his hand. "I didn't hear you."

Sol grunted. He rubbed his chin. He sighed. "Lou," he said quietly, "take the men out. I want to talk to my son for a minute. Leave the ads on the floor."

"I'm sorry," Aaron said. "I just want to discuss something with you."

Sol said irritably, "What's on your mind?"

"You mean you'll listen?"

"I'll give you a word of warning! Don't be fresh in meetings."

"It's got nothing to do with me. I'm a painter."

"What's this all about?"

"There's a girl who says she's pregnant."

Sol glared. "By you?"

"She says so."

"Congratulations. You want to marry her? A kid like you, with no prospects? Send her to Puerto Rico. One of my salesmen got a girl in trouble. Cost him six hundred, including plane fare. Where are you going to get six hundred dollars?"

"From you."

"This girl know how rich I am?"

"I don't think she wants an abortion. She wants me."

Sol waved irritably. "Who cares? It's all a matter of money. You don't have any. I'm offering you a deal. Come to work."

15

POLLY LEFT THE PHONE BOOTH and hurried to her home on lower Fifth Avenue. She had called Aaron to say she had seen Toby.

She undressed. A lassitude came over her. The room was close, the afternoon sun was unseasonably warm. Closing her eyes, she fell backwards on her unmade bed and threw her arms out at her sides in a gesture of weariness.

She brushed at her breasts and, inadvertently, her nail touched the edge of her nipple. She shivered. She did it again. Another shiver. She commenced a gentle massage of both her nipples with her thumb and forefinger. She hummed quietly and continued rubbing. As the rhythm increased, she tugged, first delicately, and then harder at her swelling nipples. She stopped humming. She clenched her teeth and pulled and squeezed with all the strength in her small hands and allowed her mind to conjure up the most primitive series of images. Ruthless Filipinos. Sadists, perverts, Arabs—old fantasies, familiar friends who had accompanied her at prep school and summer camp. Instead of increasing her pleasure, they dulled it. She thought of Aaron. A warm feeling spread down her breasts to her stomach. She thought of Toby. The warmth increased. Her fingers wandered down her stomach. They probed and investigated, and flew out of control as she grabbed at herself. Yet, even then the magic eluded her. Despite her efforts to clear her mind, the image of Aaron pleading with her broke her rhythm. She remembered Toby; a totem before his tiny mother. Her hands relaxed and fell against her thighs. Satisfaction evaded her. They seemed so helpless those two. So unerotic.

The downstairs bell rang impatiently. She wrapped a terry cloth robe about her and ran down to answer it.

Aaron glared from behind the front door window. When he saw her approach, his expression hardened. He jabbed the bell a second time.

"For Pete's sake!" he complained when she opened the door.

"Come in," she said cheerfully. "Don't be angry."

"I am."

She spoke urgently. "I did it for you. I went and saw those dreadful Ferns. On your behalf. I simply *had* to go and extricate you. Why should an artist concern himself with aggressive women who drag and pull at him?"

"Hold on."

She mussed his hair and smiled up at him. "Do I look awful in this robe?"

"You had no right!"

She said idly, "I didn't want a silly pregnant girl pestering you. You're mine. You said you were."

"You don't know me."

"You've been telling me you're in love."

"Suppose I am."

"Well?"

"It means you're mine. It doesn't mean I'm yours."

"Really," she said with annoyance. "They don't scare me. I rang the bell and walked right up to them! 'See here,' I said, 'lay off of Franklin. He's a good kid who would never do a girl in.' I was doing fine until the doctor called."

"The doctor?"

"Yes." She looked back at him over her shoulder. "A German."

"What do you mean?"

"Some psychiatrist called. Helga goes to a psychiatrist."

Aaron sat on the step, his head in his hands. "She found Dr. Brest. She's like a detective."

Polly continued climbing. At the top, she leaned on the banister and said, "Come up and keep me company. I have to get ready. Daddy's coming to take me to dinner."

"Wait," he said. "Then what happened? What did the doctor do?"

"Well, it got pretty funny around that time. The mother went sort of berserk. The idea of this doctor describing a daughter of hers as a nut—and the brother. A giant. He tried to calm the mother. She shoved him out of the way, or rather, she tried to. It was like shoving a mountain. Brother asked her not to make scenes in front of strangers, meaning me. Mother ordered me out of her house. It was the best offer I had all day."

"What did you say about me and Helga?"

"Nothing. I left. They were supposed to go to the doctor's and get your Helga. I can't imagine why. Families have strange loyalties."

She entered the bedroom.

"You can sit in here. I'll dress in the bathroom. Forgive the mess, but you see the maid disappeared when Mother died and I'm not sure why. Either she was superstitious or we owed her money. We're broke, you know. Daddy shot the whole inheritance on drink."

Polly spoke through the half-opened bathroom door as she brushed her hair, "Send her off for an abortion. I knew a girl who had an abortion once; she was my best friend. She fell madly in love with a gas station attendant, a terrible boy with large feet. He got her in trouble. She simply went off and had this abortion. She said it was practically painless."

"She doesn't want an abortion. She wants me. She wants me to marry her. It's the craziest thing I ever heard of!"

Polly peeked through the door. "No, it isn't. You're a very attractive boy."

He scowled.

"When you're angry. You like my hair this way?" She had walked out of the bathroom. Her robe was loosely belted and she kept it tight to her with both hands. Her hair was placed softly on top of her head in a dark pile.

He stood up straight. "You look like an angel. I had no idea you had such a long white neck."

"I hate my neck. That's why I wear my hair down."

He ordered: "Don't hate your neck!"

"Well, I do," she said petulantly. "Besides you don't care. You're all involved."

He breathed heavily and rushed to her, grasping her shoulders with such force, the robe opened, exposing one shoulder and her breasts.

"No," she said.

She stood on tiptoe and wrapped her arms about his neck, and as she did so, she shook loose the robe. She allowed it to fall to the floor and pressed her naked body against him. Her grip surprised him. Its quick desperation pulled him forward and, as he struggled to hold his balance, she hopped in the air and released him, so that he stumbled ahead. Stepping to the side, she watched him falling, her hands covering her nakedness. He righted himself by stiff-arming the bathroom door, but the latch gave, and he fell forward, slipping on the wet floor; his legs were bent and apart like a novice skier. A violent grab at the shower curtain prevented him from toppling into the empty bath tub.

He heard her in the bedroom trying to stifle a laugh, and when he marched back stoically, she lay on the bed, the robe around her, both hands in her open mouth and tears of laughter on her cheeks.

She looked so beautiful that he forgot his annoyance and rushed toward the bed, his arms outstretched, saying positively that he would love her always.

"I never know when to believe you."

"You can believe me," he said forcefully. "You better believe me, because I'd give up everything for you. Even my paintings. I'd live in Jackson Heights for you."

"Well, that may be," she said reflectively. "But it won't make any difference. I'm not apt to sleep with you."

"Sleep?" he exclaimed. "I want more than that. I want everything. The whole package. I want to cover you like a tent!"

"Oh," she said.

"Polly! I worship you!" And, as he spoke, his fingers worked into the opening in her robe.

"Don't," she said quietly. "I mean I'm not what you think I am. I mean I talk like I know all about everything but I'm afraid I'm a virgin."

"Now's the time," he said forcefully, standing and unbuttoning his pants.

She reflected on this. "No, I guess you better not do that.

Not now at any rate, because I want the first time to be marvelous."

"It will be!" He stepped out of his pants and stood shyly in his undershirt and turned sideways, so his nudity wouldn't frighten her.

She said sweetly, "You look awfully cute." She turned her back and parted her robe above her waist. "I hope Daddy doesn't come home."

"Polly!" he said as he leaped on the bed. "I love you."

"I don't care if you do or not," she explained. "I've held on to this virginity long enough. You're so cute you make me cry."

He yanked his shoes and socks off and removed his undershirt. He waited for her, his arms extended as she slowly turned and reached for him, the robe falling open, exposing her short white body.

"Well," she gasped. "I feel so marvelous."

"So do I," he said, surprised to find himself shouting.

"Will it hurt?" She looked fearful. "Are you going to put that all the way in?"

"Nothing hurts! It's all for us."

She gasped. "It hurts."

"I'm trying to be careful."

"Why does it hurt?"

He kissed her.

"I mean it," she said. "It's too painful." She cried once, a sharp sound that held him immobile. Then, with a shout of joy she wrapped her arms around his back and opened her wet eyes and sighed with disbelief.

"I had no idea things felt that good!" She grabbed his hair and clenched her teeth.

"Polly, I adore you!"

"Don't stop!"

Just then they heard heavy footsteps downstairs. She shoved him off her.

"Oh, no! It's Daddy. Daddy's home."

Aaron was on his feet, grabbing for his clothing. "What's he doing here?"

"He lives here, silly." Polly moved fast. She got to the bathroom and closed the door, saying, "If he comes in, act natural."

Aaron raced about collecting his clothing and cursing her father.

From downstairs the voice was a tentative bleat.

"Polly? Is that you, dear? Daddy's home."

He commenced a slow climb up the stairs. "Is someone with you?"

Polly stamped about in the bathroom and emerged momentarily, her hair brushed, lipstick in place, and her robe securely belted. Aaron, who had managed to dress himself with furious speed, stood waiting. Polly straightened the bedclothes and skipped to the door. She opened it just as Gus emerged from the stairway.

"Hi," she said pleasantly.

"Ah, Polly," he lamented. "It's been a trying day."

His hair hung damply over his forehead, his tie was loose, his jacket unbuttoned and riding back on his fat shoulders.

"If I were a drinking man, I'd be out drinking."

"I know. It's hard being without her."

"Who? Your mother? It's *impossible* without her."

"I miss her too."

"I don't. I got used to missing her. Whenever we had a real bad fight, she left me. Yet she always came back after one of our fights. This time she won't."

"Why don't you take a shower. I'll make you something to eat."

"Eat? I can't think about food." He rubbed his hand over his face and leaned for support on the banister. "What I need is a drink. I really do." He sighed. "I don't have one. (Where I get the strength God only knows.)" He peered at her in the dark hallway. "Someone in there with you? I heard voices."

She said nothing.

"I don't blame you. It's proper to see your friends at such a time. Life goes on and that sort of thing."

He placed his hands in his linen jacket pocket. "I find I have no friends. All the friends we had together. They were *her* friends."

Aaron stepped out into the hallway and stood beside Polly.

"Good afternoon, sir."

Gus regarded him blankly.

"It's you," he muttered. "It's always you. What are you doing in my daughter's bedroom?"

"He came to visit. We were chatting."

"Now I don't believe that for one minute. Who do you think you're kidding?"

His voice slurred as it grew louder. He shook his head remorsefully. "Carrying on. That's what you're doing, and Mother hardly cold in her grave."

Most forms of self-pity other than his own unnerved Aaron. "Leave her alone!"

"What?"

"You heard me. Leave her alone."

Gus clenched his teeth. "I'll pretend you never said that."

Polly comforted her father. "We'll be down in a second. Don't upset yourself."

"I'm very upset!"

"Don't protect him," Aaron said. "Protect yourself."

"He's my father!"

Gus pointed dramatically. "Get out of my house."

"Now, Daddy," she said calmly, "he came because I invited him."

Gus rocked back and forth. "Hmmm," he said sententiously, an ironic smile on his plump lips. They waited for him to speak, but he seemed to have lost track of the discussion and merely rocked and smiled.

Aaron whispered, "I think he's been drinking."

"I heard that!"

"Stop it, Aaron. He's very upset."

"I will not be insulted in my own home. If I were a younger man, I'd punch you." He lowered his large head. "I am known for my courage."

"Please," Polly cried.

Gus grinned suddenly. He folded his hands behind him and, bowing slightly from the waist, addressed Aaron with mock courtesy.

"I am now off to the nearest dispenser of potable beverages. Be good enough to leave shortly, because I don't want to find you in my daughter's bed when I return, which will be shortly. If, however, I discover you here, I shall not only call the police, but I will institute charges which will, I guarantee, hold up in any court in the land. Furthermore, if I ever again see you on my property, I will make a citizen's arrest, because, young sir, you are an ill-mannered, arrogant pup who is not worthy of his hire. ALSO—and mark this well —I will do everything in my power to keep you and Polly apart."

As he spoke he grew more agitated, and by the time he finished, he had so filled himself with outrage, that he lurched towards Aaron, his hands in front and clawlike. Just as he was about to have his face scratched, Aaron sidestepped and jumped back.

"Don't scratch Aaron," Polly cried.

16

HELGA FERN COMPARED HERSELF to the blind man whose sightless journey through subway trains guiltified the people there. She produced a similar discomfort in people she met. They recoiled from her, yet surrendered to her. She touched that cowardly spot in everyone.

Not Brest. He regarded her bleakly and considered throwing her out of his office.

"You are a sullen, unpleasant person," he said finally, after listening to forty minutes of laments. "You fill me with boredom. You must decide: You go either into deep analysis, five times a week, or you persist with your alibis and miseries. I give you the name of several doctors who will help you. If you decide to see them, good. If you refuse, I wash my hands of you. This is clear?"

She nodded. She bit her lip. Tears formed in her small eyes. "How cruel," she sighed, gripping her sneakered feet around the legs of his couch. "People should talk nice to people." She reached back and clutched the rear couch legs with her hands; she jammed her head into the leather pillow.

Spread-eagled, she regarded the ceiling and said sorrowfully, "One has grave difficulties being oversized."

"Nonsense."

"Being pregnant is no picnic."

Brest impatiently stamped out his cigar and rose from his chair. "Enough! Have you no shame?"

She shook her head. "People who are oversized have only regrets."

She watched him mistrustfully. Perspiration dropped into her eyes. Her body was wet from the exertion of hanging on. Her raincoat had torn at the armpits, her flannel skirt rode up above her bare knees, her pale hair shone with sweat.

"I have outside in my waiting room one patient. In five minutes, he will take your place."

"I was here first!"

"You are a selfish girl! Your condition is self-imposed, your victimization is operatic!"

As he opened his door to leave her, she cried out in a loud voice, "Help!"

He quickly shut the door. "You are insane? You wish to frighten the man outside?"

"I don't care," she muttered. "What about Aaron Franklin?"

"He's your friend."

"He raped me."

"You are totally rape-proof!"

The front door bell rang, a long, insistent blast. Helga released her grip. Her legs dropped to the floor. She sat up stiffly, her eyes bright and staring.

"There's Mother." She wet her dry lips with her tongue.

"Don't be so positive. It's perhaps the next patient."

"No one rings a bell like that. Only one person."

The ringing continued.

"Very impatient," he remarked mildly.

She pointed towards the door. "Hurry. Keep her waiting and she gets migraines."

Brest was interested. "It all started with that young man. A pied piper for neurotics."

He opened his door and walked slowly through his waiting room. As he appeared, a small man in a tightly buttoned double-breasted overcoat regarded him from behind a copy of the *Kenyon Review*. The man waved at him and spoke tentatively.

"Ready for me?"

"Moment," Brest grunted, continuing to cross the room. "Someone rings."

"I hear them!" the man exclaimed.

"Ya," Brest agreed. "Forgive me please, Mr. Flood, I shall be a few moments longer."

Flood closed his magazine and spoke quietly. "It's not fair to keep me waiting. My appointment was for three. It's always three on Wednesdays."

"Ya. Ya. Today, we are running behind schedule."

"I can't bear to wait."

Brest faced his patient. "Calm down, Mr. Flood. A matter of minutes."

Flood slapped the magazine against the side of his chair. "I hate you for it."

"Don't hate me, Mr. Flood."

Flood lowered his head. "All right."

Brest reached the foyer, turned on the overhead light, and opened the heavy front door, but even with the door open, the ringing continued. He stared at the woman whose fingers remained on the bell and said loudly, "Stop! I'm here." She gave the bell an extra blast and glared at him. Beside her, slightly to the rear, he saw an elegant man, clothed like a member of the Diplomatic Corps; behind him, on a lower step, was a huge handsome youth in a four-hundred-dollar silk suit and a fashionably tilted straw boater.

She spoke, "You are Brest?"

"I am."

"Where is she?"

"Where is who?"

Vernon stepped forward one measured pace. "Ah," he began politely, "our daughter is apparently inside your office. You were kind enough to phone us."

"We see your daughter now, and in a few moments I give her back to you."

Corliss sniffed at the air. She advanced across the room, her heels striking the carpet with force. Following her, and smiling sheepishly, was her husband Vernon, and finally, bringing up the rear, Toby, not sure of why he had come, his mind filled with memories of Polly Gang.

Corliss entered Brest's office speaking to her husband. "The girl had no right to see a psychiatrist before consulting her own mother. Plenty of children made mistakes. My cousin Sybil had a lover before turning eighteen—a ski instructor at Innsbruck. The family simply slipped her off to Havana. And in a week, she was back on the slopes, no worse for wear. My brother's daughter, Angela, got pregnant at college in her junior year. No one knew or cared. The girl went off to San Juan and nothing was said. The family shrugged it off. Sex is no more important than any other activity. You go in with your eyes open and you take your chances."

Helga had resumed her original pose; she gripped the couch tightly and flattened herself against the leather. She ignored her mother.

Corliss refused to greet her. Nor would she accept the chair the doctor offered.

Helga moaned. "It's all her fault. If she treated people decently—none of this would have happened."

Brest turned politely to Corliss, who narrowed her eyes and frowned. "Don't bow at me, you German."

"Now, Cor." Vernon, who had seated himself near the window, raised his arm to caution her. "Try to behave." He gazed down at poor Helga and patted her clenched fist. "There, there, dear girl. It will be all right. Your mother and brother and I are here to help you, as I'm sure the doctor is. We're on your side."

Toby nodded with detachment and agreed with Vernon. "Don't worry," he said quietly. "Everything will be fine." He looked at his hands, a vague smile on his suntanned face.

Helga said: "People don't need her around."

"Wait!" Brest said. "I specifically invited them. How else could I get you to move?"

"Nothing will make me move!"

Brest sighed. "Then, I call the police."

Helga slowly rose from the couch and, sitting straight up, clenched her hands in her lap and talked directly at the far wall, staring fixedly as if she were reading an eye chart.

"He attacked me," she said in a detached monotone. "It was a college weekend. At this dance, he invited me out for a walk. I said all right, because he seemed decent and good looking. A smooth talker. Someone that one could trust. Not like some men one meets in Southampton. One never found out, of course, because the thing happened to one so quickly, with such violence, that one simply shut one's eyes and hoped for the blessed relief of fainting. No such luck. He attacked one over and over, thrusting his, you know, in one repeatedly. One was afraid to cry out for fear of being expelled on the spot. They never believe one, people in charge. They just expel one." She sighed. "Well, that's what happened. And now one finds oneself heavy with child and friendless." She dropped her head and sobbed in her hands.

In the shocked silence, Corliss' voice sounded harsh and menacing. "The girl's lying."

Brest shrugged his plump shoulders. "Perhaps. We stop now. We continue tomorrow."

Vernon said, "How awful for you, child. Why didn't you tell us immediately?"

"Too ashamed," she mumbled falling against him. She hugged his thin body, and, placing her face against his pocket handkerchief, sobbed deeply.

Toby had not been listening.

"Brothers should help," she was saying. "Brothers should find the man and horsewhip him."

Impatiently Toby said, "What's the fellow's name?"

"Don't hurt him!" Helga cried.

Brest slapped his desk top. "Now we stop."

Toby stood and beamed at them and seemed so cheerful among the long tense faces around him that he self-consciously covered his face and forced an expression of solemn concern. However, his mind was on Polly. His body ached as if from a bad cold; his joints seemed raw and feverish; his stomach churned nervously. Yet, he had never felt more alert or adventuresome; never had his future seemed so filled with rich promise. He imagined her dear, sweet face against his own. He tasted her mouth, he engulfed her small body and joyously lifted her onto his chest. She would be his! Hadn't she smiled? Hadn't she squeezed his arm on leaving his house?

Someone was ringing the outside bell. Brest left his office door open. Excusing himself, he reentered his waiting room. Flood saw him.

"Another patient, eh, Doctor? Sure. Forget Flood. What the hell! Who is Flood?"

"Moment, Mr. Flood."

He opened his front door and blinked. A familiar figure stood there.

"Hello, Max," the man said in perfect German. "I'm most inconsiderate, I know, barging in during office hours, but I was in the neighborhood and, well, I hoped I'd catch you for a moment between visits."

Brest was delighted. He grabbed the man's hand and pumped it joyously. "My God! Archie Fellows!" He laughed and looked up at him. "My good friend!"

"Well, I hope so. After you hear what I came to ask you, you might change your mind."

"So?"

"Come out on the step. I can tell you in confidence."

Fellows spoke quickly. "Look, Max. I sent a young student to you named Aaron Franklin. Rather I gave him your name. That was weeks ago. Then his father got sick. Now he's disappeared. I called his father's office and was informed that they have no knowledge of his whereabouts. It sounds fishy to me. I suspect the boy is wandering around New York, and I was wondering, if he does call you, you would do me the kindness of letting me know. I hate to trouble you with a favor like this, knowing how busy you are, but there's a faint chance he will look you up. His father wants him to quit college and go to work in his business—some sort of ladies' undergarments—and is, therefore, keeping the boy's whereabouts a secret."

"Nu? Just another student."

"No," Fellows said solemnly. "A big talent. The boy is apparently under the father's influence, and I simply cannot let a talent like this dissipate itself in the ladies' underwear business. I have convinced the school authorities to give him a complete scholarship. I mean, look, Max. A good one comes along so rarely."

Brest smiled. "Your troubles are over. I have met this genius. He comes to me as a patient."

Fellows clapped him on the back. "Good old Max!"

"Already he has one girl pregnant. She saw him on Fifty-seventh Street and says she fell in love with him. Quick. She follows him on this train. She gets off when he does. She discovers where he sleeps in his college and seduces him. At least this is my diagnosis."

"Amazing!"

Brest agreed.

"Can you analyze him?"

Brest shrugged.

"When is his next appointment?"

Just then, a loud noise inside his house interrupted the doctor. He turned. He opened the front door in time to see a Bauhaus easy chair overturn. "Halt!" he ordered, rushing forward.

Fellows ran in behind him. The sight of his friend trying to restore order in what appeared to be a mob of people angered him. A large handsome youth had lifted a tiny man in a winter overcoat up in the air and was holding him on a level with the mantelpiece. Behind him stood an elderly woman clutching her head. An extremely tall plain girl loomed in the doorway, holding on to a distinguished man.

Brest shouted: "Put him down. He's a patient!"

The little man waved his overcoated arms and kicked out with his pointed shoes. But, as he was held at arm's length, his kicks struck the wall and dislodged a painting.

Brest cried, "A Nolde!"

The picture rocked, became unhooked, and would have

struck the floor if Fellows hadn't run forward with two long strides and caught it. He held it to him and eyed the man in the silk suit.

"That's about enough," he said, panting from the exertion. "I'm damn near seventy, but I'll smack you with a poker if your horseplay continues. You might have damaged this picture."

"And me!" Flood said.

He was placed onto the floor where he righted his overcoat and said, with dignity, "It was all in fun, rather." He held out his hand to his attacker. "I'm Vincent Flood."

Toby, who had grabbed him and held him in the air, wasn't ready to introduce himself. "This person insulted Mother." He pointed dramatically at Corliss. "That woman there."

Fellows rehung the picture. "You had no right to destroy a man's possessions."

"Return my chair," Brest said loudly, "to its original position. Then take your family completely out of my office."

17

WHEN GUS LEFT THEM ALONE, they went immediately to the kitchen and prepared lunch. "We have hours," Polly assured him, holding his hand. "He won't be back. I know him. Once he hits the bars."

Aaron offered her a piece of orange. He had found half of a watermelon, two tomatoes, and a loaf of bread in the refrigerator. He placed them on the kitchen table and divided the food.

"I'm starved," she announced. "I had no idea it would be so much fun!"

He said meaningfully: "I think I love you."

"I would hope so!"

"I would do anything for you." He stood and walked behind her chair. He wrapped his arms around her breasts and kissed the top of her hair.

"I do like that, but let's first eat. I've been playing Ping-Pong and running all over town."

"I wonder if the brother knows. About me and his sister."

"I hope not. He's a first-rate athlete. He almost beat me in Ping-Pong and I'm pretty good."

"Ping-Pong is no test."

They consumed all the food in the icebox. They then searched the cupboards and kitchen closet and found a half-eaten box of Ritz crackers, anchovies, two cans of salmon, a bottle of black olives, maraschino cherries, some preserved peaches, and a jar of cocktail onions.

"We normally eat in restaurants," Polly said, opening the cans on the wall opener. "Even when Mother was alive. There was never food in the house."

The phone rang. He dropped the empty anchovy can and felt a sharp pain as the tin cut the skin on his bare left foot. He grabbed it and lifted it. The cut was a minor one, yet a few drops of blood formed and mixed with the olive oil from the can. He called to her to get adhesive tape.

She had gone to the living room to answer the phone, and he heard her talking. "No. No." She seemed agitated. "It's completely out of the question."

She clapped her hand over the phone and whispered, "It's the brother, Toby. He wants to see me."

Toby hadn't known what to expect when he discovered her number and dialed it. His hands perspired so the dial skidded under his finger. He redialed. When she answered, he was too tense to speak. He simply blurted out his name and asked if she would see him. She said no with such finality that his shoulders sagged. He was determined, however, to keep her on the phone.

"It was quite a scene," he reported, speaking rapidly. "We went. All three of us. To this Dr. Brest. It was quite a mess. When we got there, some man in the doctor's waiting room took an instant dislike to Mother. I remember that you didn't care much for her either, so perhaps what I'm going to tell you will amuse you. He insulted her. He called her a domineering old bitch." He paused and asked uncertainly, "What do you think?"

Polly couldn't answer. She was laughing.

"Don't hang up," he said. "There's more."

"Great! I'm still here. What did Helga do?"

"Poor Helga. She looked terrible. Even for her. Her raincoat was ripped and her dress was stained. She had been crying, as usual, and her eyes were swollen and red. Her hair was all askew and she had sneakers on. I never really cared much for her when we were little, and even now, I don't find her much fun. But, after all, when your own sister is made pregnant by some smooth-talking artist, it's enough to make your blood boil. His name is Aaron Franklin. He must be taught a lesson. The fellow is no good. He's the worst kind of guy. I'm not saying he ought to marry her, but he should be with her and help her decide what to do. . . . Today, nothing affected me, really. You know why nothing affects me, because I think I love you, Polly. I know it sounds dumb, but it's the truth. I swear it. You're on my mind. You're all I think about. And at first it puzzled me, because we only just met; and then I said the hell with it. A man can't always control his emotions. I mean, just because I look like an athlete it doesn't mean I don't experience things. And I certainly experienced you. You were so beautiful standing in my doorway I thought my heart would stop beating. I can't recall ever seeing so beautiful a girl. So you'll have to forgive me for carrying on like this." He took a deep breath. "I'm through talking. I'm going to act. I'm coming down. I won't be more than ten minutes."

In amazement, she heard the phone click. She stared at it. Finally, she turned to Aaron, the dead phone in her hand.

"Stop hopping around, Aaron. It's only a little scratch."

"Who was that?"

"On the phone?"

"Yes."

She smiled mysteriously. "You'll never guess."

"What's his name?"

"That's the funny part. His name."

"My foot hurts. Who was on the phone?"

She cleared her throat. "Well, it's your future brother-in-law. It appears he doesn't want you at all. He wants me."

"Impossible!" Aaron stood and limped toward her. "You belong to me! I've told you that."

"I know," she said idly. "But he doesn't know it." She crossed her legs. "He'll be here soon."

"What do you mean, here! You're letting him come here? I thought we were going back to bed."

"I couldn't stop him. He simply announced the fact and hung up."

He protested. "Lock the door."

"I can't lock it. Daddy always loses his keys. Especially when he's drinking. Let's fix your foot. Then I have to get some clothes on."

"Never mind my foot. Lock the door."

"Suit yourself," she said airily and proceeded up the stairs to her bedroom. "And I suggest you put your shoes and socks on. And brush your hair."

"For him?"

"No. For me. I don't want the world to know we've been to bed."

"We haven't! Not really."

"Anyway, it doesn't look right. Please hurry."

"My foot prevents it."

"Ye God!" She stamped up the stairs, robe swinging wildly above her plump bottom.

18

TOBY TREMBLED in the phone booth. The floor shook with his elation. He had done it! For twenty-two years he had smiled and held doors for people, had ushered at weddings, had referred to older men as "sir" and generally comported himself like a hotel doorman. It was a matter of training, he knew. Boys in his class, raised by nannies, tortured by headmasters one hundred miles from home, developed eccentric habits. It was as if a needle had been inserted at the first preparatory school, and all valor had been drained out, so that, after Groton and Dartmouth and Harvard and a job downtown, there was, wandering around New York, an entire generation of eunuchs.

He smacked his hands together and joyfully left the booth and walked smartly toward Polly's, proud and triumphant. Footsteps behind him grew more pronounced. He turned. Seeing Flood, his overcoat buttoned against some personal blizzard, he greeted him happily.

"What in hell do you want?"

Flood frowned. "Talking to me?"

"Yes. I'm talking to you, little fellow."
"Oh, it's you. The chap from before."
"You know very well it is. You've been following me."
"You've got to be joking. Why would I do that?"
"I have no idea. Because you're demented, I guess."
"That's tactless."
"Look! You insulted my mother. A man doesn't do that to someone's mother unless he's pretty peculiar."
"Being peculiar is hardly demented. I mean, only crazy people are so characterized."
"Yes. Well, I have to see someone, so go away."
"Let's be friends."
"Sure. Why not. After all, you didn't actually hurt her."
"Let's have lunch some day."
"I don't think so."
Flood gazed up at him, blocked his way. "How can you stand such a person for a mother?"
"Out of the way, or I'll lift you and move you."
"I like it when you lift me."
"Then I'll hit you. Would you like that?"
"It depends where you hit me. And how hard."
"I'm not kidding." Toby brushed him to the side with a quick shove and strode off rapidly. Soon, however, he heard the footsteps gaining on him. He lowered his head and commenced running, dashing against the lights, dodging cars and sprinting along the sidewalks. After a few blocks, he slowed and looked back. Aside from some housewives and delivery boys, he saw no one. He began walking the remaining four blocks, when up ahead, he saw Flood grinning shyly.
"You must be a track man."
"I simply hailed a cab. You see, I know what direction you're going. I heard you on the phone."
"You mean you eavesdropped?"

"Don't be ridiculous. I happened to be passing, and I recognized your voice. So I paused."

"Why aren't you at the doctor's?"

Flood yawned. "I decided not to be analyzed anymore. After all, I'm a human being."

At that time, inside Polly's bedroom, Aaron stared morosely out the window. "Someone's coming," he announced. "Two men. A big one and a little one."

"It must be Brother," she said. "I'm not nearly ready."

"I won't let them in."

"But you have to. I promised. You might like him. He's quite nice."

"If he's anything like old Helga, he's no friend of mine." He glowered down at them. "Who's the guy with him? Some little person in an overcoat."

"How should I know?" She struggled into a brassiere.

"They must be friends," he noted. "Because Brother seems to be lifting him in the air."

Polly emerged, her strap undone, the robe thrown about her shoulders like a cape. "Aaron, if you're fooling around, I'll be angry." She looked out onto the street. "Oh! That's Brother all right. Who is he lifting?"

Down in the street, Toby had his hands full. He finally grabbed Flood's collar with one hand and, clutching the seat of the coat with the other, propelled him down the walk. Toby rushed to Polly's door and, finding it open, jumped inside, slamming it shut behind him.

"Hello," he called breathlessly. "Polly, are you home?"

She whispered to Aaron: "Go down and introduce yourself and put him in the living room."

"I'm staying with you."

"He's perfectly harmless."

She called out pleasantly: "Hi, Toby. Go in the living room. I'll be right down."

"Polly!" he shouted joyfully. He bounded up the stairs.

Aaron blocked his way. "Hold on, fellow. She's not dressed."

"Who in hell are you?"

"A family friend."

"Whoever you are, out of the way."

"You'll have to wait."

"Polly," he called. "Where are you?"

"I'm here, Toby. Please go downstairs, and, Aaron, you go with him."

Toby gripped the banister. His jaw stiffened. He widened his eyes. "What nerve. What have you got to say for yourself?"

"About what?"

"You know what."

"Give me a hint."

"And what are you doing here?"

"I might ask you the same thing."

"Look," Toby said grimly. "Don't play games with me. That kind of cheap stuff might work with helpless girls, but I am not impressed."

He advanced slowly. At the top of the stairs, they faced each other. Although they were the same height, Toby was fifty pounds heavier. Aaron retreated one step. "I can't hit you," he warned. "I need my hands for painting. . . . Stay away from Polly!"

He faced Toby from a safe distance.

Toby stood still, his face red with fury.

Aaron struck him. His fist landed square on the bigger man's nose. Then he backed up, his eye on the front door, prepared to make a run for it.

He spoke breathlessly as blood spurted down Toby's nostrils. "Do you get my meaning?"

The force of the blow knocked Toby against the banister. It sagged, then gave way. Only the fact that he reached out and grabbed Aaron's arm prevented him from falling backward to the floor below. His blood covered them both. Aaron struggled to free himself and, in doing so, they both fell to the carpet.

"Damn you!" Toby exclaimed, astonished at the lack of fair play. "You've broken my nose." And he cracked Aaron in the ribs with a flurry of short left hooks that knocked the wind out. Aaron collapsed, gasping for breath. Toby raised his fist to finish off the job, when suddenly, with a banging of doors and a clatter of feet on the steps, a small form hurtled itself between them. It was Flood, his overcoat flapping about his thin ankles, who saved Aaron from getting his teeth knocked out. In an effort to join in and help with the pummeling, he shoved Toby backwards.

"Two against one," Aaron cried, regaining his breath.

Toby swept Flood to the side with a short shove and prepared to smash Aaron when Polly shouted: "Stop it! All of you. Are you all crazy?"

Flood said, "Who is she?" and stood up. He rearranged his collar and belt and cautioned Toby. "You better stop now, or your nose will be ruined."

Straddling Aaron and dripping blood on him, Toby spoke gruffly. "Get me a towel and some ice to keep the swelling down."

Aaron protested. "Get him off me, Polly."

"Shut up," Toby snapped. "I'm not finished with you."

"I'm finished with you. You and your little friend." He twisted his face and glared at Polly. "And I'm through with you, too. I'm a painter, not a street fighter."

Polly tugged at Toby's shoulder. "Get up now. We better get you into the bathroom and take care of your face."

"How about me? I have an infected foot and some broken ribs."

Polly stared at them and said hopelessly, "This is awful!"

"I agree," Flood said rushing forward with a silk handkerchief. "I've never seen a boy with a more perfect nose."

Polly frowned. "Who are you supposed to be?"

"Merely a friend of the victim. What have you done to him?"

"Get away from here!" Toby slowly stood and gripped his nose. "I mean it, Flood. I've had enough of you for one day."

"Don't turn on me. I came to help."

Polly's attempt at solicitude failed. She bit her lip and covered her mouth with her hands. She giggled. "What a perfectly marvelous overcoat."

Aaron moaned. Holding his sides, he forced himself to stand. "There was no need to break any ribs."

Toby said nasally, "I'm covered with blood."

"Is that girl actually laughing at my overcoat?"

"Shut up, Flood. Get away from me."

"I thought we were friends!"

"You thought wrong!"

"Come," Polly said, controlling her voice. "Come in the bathroom." She took Toby's arm and led him down the hall to her bedroom.

The front door opened. It was Gus Gang, drunk and disheveled.

"Polly," he called, squinting up at them. "It's Daddy. Daddy's home."

He advanced clumsily up the stairs. "What in heaven's name has happened to the banister?" He looked about him at the bloodied rug. "What foulness!"

"I'm in here, Daddy," Polly called pleasantly. "Be out in a sec. Soon as I wash old Toby's face."

"I say, Polly. That's a bit thick. I mean, a chap goes out for a drink and finds his only daughter half naked, entertaining three men."

Flood turned to Aaron. "He's right, you know. Fair's fair."

19

"GANGRENE IS NOT A POSSIBILITY."

Dr. Crowl closed his black bag, nodded his old head, and cleared his throat.

"In these cases, we recommend rest, plenty of liquids, and sulfa. As for the ribs, I've done all I can. Ribs are quite capable of healing themselves. I've taped them. Aside from some general discomfort and a desire to itch himself under the adhesive tape, the boy will be good as new." He rubbed his chin. "It must have been a peculiar fight. Ribs I understand. But why should they puncture his foot?"

Aaron observed his mother and father standing at the foot of his bed. He lay wrapped in tape in the bedroom of his studio.

Sol said, "You heard the doctor. Rest."

"Why are you shouting?" Alma asked. "The boy's in pain."

"How did it happen?" Sol asked.

"He's too weak to talk."

"The time has come for talking."

Aaron eyed his swollen foot. "Two guys jumped me. It was a total surprise."

"What did you do?"

"I broke the guy's nose."

He added judiciously, "He got in a few good ones afterwards. I was lucky to get out alive. I never saw a man so big and so angry both at the same time." He stared intently at his father. "This guy is the brother of you-know-who. He was like an avenging angel."

Sol nodded knowingly. "He has every right to be angry."

Alma pulled at his sleeve. "What's going on? What are you both keeping from me?"

"Nothing," Sol said. "He needs his rest."

"Suddenly he needs his rest. What's going on here?"

"I'll explain later."

Alma's look of concern deepened. Lines formed on her forehead. Her small mouth puckered as if to whistle. "What, what?" she stammered.

Aaron flopped over on his side and propped his head on his hand. The sheets against his foot made it throb.

"It's like this. I got a girl pregnant and to tell you the truth, I don't really remember doing it. And, in the meantime, I haven't done any serious painting."

"My God! I'm dying!"

Sol said, "There's plenty of time for pictures."

"No!" he shouted, sitting up. "Everyone says that. The thing is, there isn't ever enough time."

Sol said, "Don't be fresh."

"Do you realize what it means to make a picture? It's impossible! No one can do it. That's the whole thing! Nobody ever made a perfect painting, and that includes Titian and Giotto and Goya and Bellini. They can't bring it off. It simply can't be done. Some come close, that's all. So, when something is totally beyond the reach of human beings, then you've got to admire the man who sets out to try. It takes a whole lifetime. Don't bother me about pregnant girls and the ladies' underwear business. My eye is on the main chance."

He turned on his stomach and sunk his head in the pillow.

Sol turned to his wife. "Who said anything about the underwear business?"

20

EVERYONE AGREED: Toby Fern was a fine-looking boy. In Palm Beach, Southampton, and in town, mothers had their eye on him.

The amazing thing about his nose was its perfection. It had the thin firm purposefulness of noses in Greek statuary, an idealized shape, an unattainable structure; so when Aaron broke it, it altered his style.

Polly noticed the change. They met a day after the fight in a midtown restaurant.

She said, "Your nose. It has a bump."

"Where is Franklin?"

"In bed, poor dear. His foot is infected."

"He's got a bad character."

Polly tilted her head. "I've just noticed. You're not blushing!"

He stared at her evenly. "I've outgrown it."

She held out her hand. "Congratulations."

He shook it. "Thanks," he said formally. "To me it's one vast relief."

At that time Aaron was in bed. He spoke twice to Polly. Although he telephoned repeatedly, she was usually out.

"You fool no one with your Southern accent," her father said. "I know you for what you are. I'm sending you a bill for a broken banister. Two hundred and fifty bucks!"

The phone crashed.

Aaron telegraphed: UNABLE TO REACH YOU. FIND IT STRANGE YOU DON'T CALL.

Early that evening Polly arrived. She carried an armful of autumn flowers.

"Hi, sport," she said, dropping them on the bed.

"Polly!" he shouted, sitting up. The sudden effort pained him. "Help me up!"

Placing an arm behind him she raised him to a sitting position.

"You poor dear. You really are in pain."

"That oaf hits hard."

"You broke his nose."

Aaron viewed her with suspicion. "It seems to me you know a lot about him."

"I only went to his house once. To see your Helga."

"She's not mine!"

"You did sleep with her."

"She isn't my Helga."

"Don't raise your voice. She's carrying your child!"

She reached for a pad next to his bed. The top sheet of paper was filled with a large brown and blue picture.

"I love this."

"It's not finished."

"Who's the fat man?"

"It isn't finished."

"Don't be a pill, Aaron. Who's the fat man playing the piano?"

"I made it up."

"Suit yourself. I think it's awfully good. It's the first thing of yours I've seen."

"I have lots more in another room," he said expansively. "Care to look?"

"I'd love to, but I have to get back to the city."

"You just got here!"

"I know."

"Then stay!"

"I can't tonight. Daddy expects me. Suppose I come back tomorrow."

"How did you come? Do you own an automobile?"

She paused. "Look, you might as well know. I borrowed a car from a friend . . . a Massaratti."

"What kind of car?"

"You don't see too many Massarattis on the road."

"That's true."

"Well, how about it?"

"Is it a Massaratti?"

"It's nothing to be ashamed of."

"I know: I just want to hear you admit it."

"Admit what?"

"That it's a Massaratti. They're very expensive."

"I haven't any idea what they cost."

"They cost plenty."

"What about it?"

"Nothing. Only your so-called friend must think a lot of you to lend you a ten-thousand-dollar automobile."

"What do you mean by that?"

"Who is this man? Do I know him?"

"You broke his nose."

"Fern!"

"Well, I'll be going."

"Don't dent the car."

"I have no intention of denting the car."

"When are you coming back?"

"First thing in the morning."

She reached for him. She placed her arms about him and kissed his forehead. As he attempted to hold her, she withdrew and cautioned him: "Don't hurt your ribs."

"You could spend the night."

"It's Daddy. I lied to him. I told him I was going to a movie. If he knew I was seeing you, he'd have a fit."

His bandaged foot throbbed relentlessly, and obstructed his vision. A round sightless lump encased in gauze, it cast its own shadow.

She reached out to him. "There, there." She placed her fingers in his hair and shook his head. She sat closer. "You'll be up in no time."

He pressed down on his sheets and shoved them forward. He swung his legs laboriously over the edge of the bed. Standing unsteadily, his arms close to his sides, he limped toward the door and opened it. "I intend confronting Toby Fern. I'm through being a cripple!"

She watched him. "You're in your pajamas."

"You're right!"

"Are you sure you should be up?"

"I've never been surer."

She shrugged. "That's all well and good, but what about your clothes?"

"She hid them. My mother."

She clapped her hands happily. "We'll drive to my house. I'll get some of Daddy's clothes for you."

She tucked one hand under his arm and helped him down the stairs.

Their progress was impeded by Mr. and Mrs. Franklin.

"He's trying to kill me," his mother said.

Sol Franklin wore his dark city clothes. He removed his panama hat when he saw Polly.

"I came in on the eight-fourteen. She said you were in constant pain." He examined his wife carefully. "So I gave up an all-night meeting. Who's the girl? A registered nurse?"

Aaron spoke brightly. "This is Polly Gang, a friend of mine."

"He comes home with cracked ribs and possible gangrene, and he wants to introduce me to people. He wants me dead." Alma Franklin held out her hand and patted Polly's arm. "You look like a nice girl."

Sol bowed and advanced. "I've heard a lot about you, young lady."

"Thank you. I'm trying to get old Aaron on his feet. Doesn't do to lie about."

"She knows more than Dr. Crowl! He should be in bed."

Sol said, "He'll be okay. I think he's in good hands." Turning to Polly, he beamed. "Had supper?"

"You're very sweet, but I must get back."

"Good," Alma said. "Go upstairs, young man." She scowled at her husband. "Don't say I didn't warn you if he limps for the rest of his life."

Sol opened the door for Polly with a sweeping gesture. "Sorry you can't stay, young lady. You sure brighten up rooms."

"See you tomorrow." She blew Aaron a kiss. "Onward and upward."

Alma spoke in a bewildered voice. "Hiding his clothes was no solution."

Sol watched Polly walk down the gravel to her car. He shook his head in admiration. "There's a looker! The kid's got a good eye."

"He also has a bad foot."

Aaron slept until late morning, when a knock on his door awakened him. It was Sol. He seemed uncomfortably burdened and clasped and unclasped his small hands as he shifted weight and tentatively appraised his son.

"Listen," he said uneasily. "I want to tell you something."

Aaron waited. When Sol cleared his throat and wet his lips and still remained silent, he urged him to continue.

"Go ahead!"

"I got ahold of Lou Lax this morning and we went to a museum. It was slow today. Nothing much doing. So listen. Let me tell you. We went to this museum, Lou Lax and me. We got into a taxi and told the cabby to take us to the biggest museum in the city. Which he did. And we went in and walked around just looking at the pictures there. It's a beautiful place. The building, I mean. Well lit, air conditioned, a very modern building. Well, I remembered what you said about all those painters. You made a certain amount of sense, for you. Anyway, we looked at those pictures, one after the other for maybe an hour, and you know something?"

Aaron shook his head.

"You know what I thought about all those pictures? I'll tell you. I didn't like them."

"None of them?"

Sol shrugged. "Why should I lie to you? I wanted to like them. I went in there in the proper frame of mind. I turned to Lou Lax. 'What do you think?' I asked him. 'Search me,' he said. 'I don't like them,' I said. 'Neither do I,' he said. 'Let's get the hell out of here.' And we did. They had pictures of naked women there I wouldn't take to bed if you held a gun at my head. And a lot of rotten fruit."

"Look," Aaron said stiffly, "I didn't ask you to go to a

museum. I'm not trying to sell you anything. You or Lou Lax."

"You strike me as a bright kid, and I'll be damned if I can see why you want to paint."

"Are you going to tell me about the business again?"

"Everybody has to earn a living."

"Painters aren't supposed to make money. Painters make paintings."

Sol sighed. God had given him a fresh kid.

21

TAPED AND LIMPING, Aaron rang Polly's doorbell at seven in the morning.

"Polly!" he shouted, "I'm here!"

"I'm coming down."

"I'm coming up!"

He stood outside her bedroom and glared at her as she covered herself with a sheet.

She yawned. "I'll have to get some clothes on."

"Stop seeing Toby Fern!"

She rubbed her eyes with her fists. "Speak quietly. I'm half asleep."

He continued, "I have certain rights."

"I'm completely undressed. I'm not wearing a nightgown or anything."

"That's no concern of mine!"

"Well, that may be, but you'll have to wait in the hall while I put something on."

"I've already seen you naked."

A pillow suddenly materialized in front of his face. As he

raised his arms to avoid it, he saw her flash past and rush to the bathroom. Snatching the pillow, he fired it after her, where it hit the closing door and forced it open. He saw her there, covering her nakedness behind a towel. She stood knock-kneed and bent over, giggling. He refused to go along with the joke.

"None of your tricks," he informed her. "Just answer some questions. Are you friendly with Toby Fern?"

She shook her head and, with her free hand, brushed her thick hair from her forehead.

"Of course not, silly. He's just someone I know."

"You do love me?"

"Suppose I do, there's no need to raise your voice."

"I haven't much time. I want to clear up a few things here. I'm off to see Helga. No more dodging her around corners. I'll track her down."

Polly looked so pretty and desirable, with the towel wrapped around her, sitting on the edge of the bathtub, so disheveled and sleepy, her bare feet turned inward and vulnerable, that he momentarily forgot himself and took a step towards her.

"What do you say?" he repeated, his voice less strident.

"I say this." Her lowered face examined her bent knees. "You frighten me."

Unnoticed, the towel slipped to the floor. She sat nakedly. "You're selfish. It simply isn't right, waking me up this early. I have a life too. I'm a person."

"I'm trying to be something with my life. Most people duck their heads and die."

She leaned forward and gathered the towel. She draped it around her.

"Well, that's true, I guess. Honestly, I don't know what to tell you."

"What's your answer? Do you love me?"
"Probably."
"Will you be here when I'm finished with Helga?"
She nodded.

22

IN HER THIRTY-BY-FIFTY GARDEN, secluded from the street by a high brick wall, Corliss Fern labored happily, carrying a basket of gardening tools, her hands encased in floppy cotton gloves, safe from Helga's whining, Toby's camaraderie, and the anxious hands of her husband.

The outside phone rang.

"Hello," she said.

"Good morning. Is Mrs. Fern up?"

"Who is this?"

"My name is Aaron Franklin, an acquaintance of Helga's."

"It's entirely too early to call!"

"You are Mrs. Fern."

"That is none of your business." She grabbed her pruning shears and waved them in the air.

"I'm coming over to see you."

"State your business."

"I want to see Helga."

She said icily: "I doubt if you'll get past the front door."

She hung up and decided not to mention the call. She returned to the garden whistling a popular tune from the twenties.

Helga joined her, wearing a flannel skirt and a blue Brooks shirt.

"Hi," she said glumly.

Her mother grunted and pruned a rosebush.

Helga pointed to a slight bulge. "The baby's growing."

Corliss looked bleakly at her daughter's stomach. "Gas. Go in the house."

"People are unsympathetic."

"You're making a general nuisance of yourself."

"People are mean."

Corliss removed her cotton gloves and tossed them in her basket. She straightened her back, stretched, and regarded her daughter.

"You washed your face." She nodded pleasantly. "You look like a real person. Keep up the good work."

She led the way to the house. There, in the hallway, Vernon and Toby, who were about to enter the dining room, intercepted them.

"Ah," she said, seeing her husband's freshly shaved face, his silk scarf and silk robe. "The late Vernon Fern."

Vernon smiled uneasily at this family joke and said: "Good morning, Hellie. Good morning, Cor."

"Had he lived, your father would have been a handsome man."

Helga said glumly, "Leave Daddy alone."

"Don't mind her," Vernon said.

Toby advanced cheerfully. "Morning, all." He pointed to Helga's stomach. "How's my nephew?"

"This house is devoid of compassion."

Vernon placed his arm around his daughter. He examined her blond hair. Usually it hung lankly about her ears. Today it shone brightly. Someone had shaped it and worked it, so that it rested gently about her face, softening the Eskimo-like wideness.

"You look lovely, my dear. Never better."

Even Toby gave her a suspicious glance. "What happened? You've changed."

Helga placed both hands on her belly. "No one's perfect."

A loud pounding on the front door halted further discussion.

"I'll go," Corliss said firmly.

"Let one of the servants." Vernon wanted his breakfast.

"I've fired the servants."

She marched to the heavy front door and yanked it open. Aaron stood on the doorstep dressed in yellow corduroy pants, a pink turtleneck sweater, and blue sneakers. He held a large package wrapped in brown paper.

She looked up. "Are you Franklin?"

"Where is she?"

"Easy, fellow," she warned. "Keep a grip on yourself." Taking his arm, she turned him so that the morning sun, which had kept his face in shadow, shone directly on him.

"I know you!" she announced.

He in turn, recognized her. "It's you. The lady in the limousine."

"Right!" She shook his hand. "And you! Well, how have you been?"

"Not so fast. Even if I know you, it won't help. I'm going to speak to your daughter and your son. They follow me. They breathe up my air!"

She gestured towards the living room. "While you're at it, speak to my husband."

"I have no fight with your husband."

Toby appeared, blocking his path.

"What do you want, Franklin? Speak quickly and get out of here before I lose my temper."

"I am not throwing the first punch."

Vernon appeared.

Helga waited in the parlor doorway. She primped her hair; she smoothed her skirt front. "Hi."

Her neatly scrubbed look surprised him. He returned to Toby. The poor man was staring at Corliss, waiting for a signal, a command.

Preparatory to insulting them all, he filled his narrow chest with air, yet words would not come and the breath eased out with impotence.

Corliss urged him on. "Go on, Franklin!"

He gazed at her and shook his head. "It's no use. I expected a fair fight."

She agreed. "Look at them. What can a person do except feel guilty?" She reached up and clapped his shoulder. "You're all right, Franklin."

"I have," Helga lamented, "this child." She indicated her stomach. "It's his child. I expect we'll marry."

"I will never marry you. You're the most depressed person I've ever seen."

"People get depressed when they're pregnant."

"Do it on your own time."

"Well said, Franklin."

Vernon said, "I'm going to breakfast. Please excuse me."

"See here, Helga. Something must be done." He took her arm. "The child is growing in your stomach. I can see a bulge there."

"Aren't you pleased?"

"No." He spoke briskly. "I haven't much time. I'm here to talk about the baby. Since it's such a burden to you, and since you refuse an abortion, I'll take it."

"Take what?" she wailed. "My baby?"

"Right. I'll take him and raise him myself. I'll hire some woman at the college to feed him, and I'll keep him in my room. Don't worry about money. I'll sell enough paintings to support him."

She protested. "Don't forget the mother!"

"You don't want the kid, Helga. I do. He's mine. I want him."

Her eyes filled. "You mean you won't even marry me?"

"There's no chance of that. Just have the kid. I'll pick him up at the hospital."

"Why won't you marry me?"

He said patiently, "You're not ugly, Helga. You're just tall."

"I'll force you to marry me. I'll go to court!"

"I've made you a generous offer. I'll keep the kid and your worries are over."

"What kind of person do you take me for?"

"All I want is the boy!"

She spoke: "I had expected the worst. I have managed to receive a bit of misery from every corner of experience." She regarded him and spoke evenly. "The baby stays with its mother."

"No need to explain," Toby said. "Say the word and I'll throw him out."

"Leave us alone," she said curtly.

"Yes, Fern. It's my child, after all."

"And what do you propose to do about it?"

Helga said stoutly, "We'll work it out without your help."

"That child will come to no good," Corliss said. "Can't you take charge?" She spoke to her husband and answered her own question. "No! Not likely. Well, we have a pregnant daughter on our hands."

"Perhaps the boy should marry her."

"That one? Not a chance!"

"Ah. I see what you mean."

"I doubt that."

"There is no need for bickering."

"Due to your lavish contributions, an entire wing has been built at the Northampton County Hospital. At the time, I considered it a waste of money. A few thousand would have been more than enough. They are in your debt, and doctors are as greedy as anyone else."

"What are you suggesting?" Vernon took two steps backward.

"Oh," she said airily. "It's perfectly simple. You arrange for an adoption. Under the most ideal circumstances. In that way, the problem *is* solved."

Toby stood up. "That goes against my grain! Besides, Franklin should marry her. After the baby's born, we can buy him off. He'd welcome the money."

"That's a bit thick. Adoption."

"Yes. Well, arrange it!"

Helga's posture changed. She stood erect. Her wide face shone with a feverish color. She thrust back her heavy shoulders. The enormity of her decision so captured her, that she stamped her feet. She flexed her muscled arms and blinked rapidly. "Mother!" she cried. "I've decided! I'm really too young to marry."

"I agree."

"So," she said, the words stumbling over each other in her eagerness to impart information. "I've decided to keep it. The child. I want it. People have a right to keep what's theirs."

"And where will you house an illegitimate baby?"

"That's just it," she cried triumphantly. "Here. With you!" Her eyes darted about. "We'll raise it together. You and I. We won't leave you, Mother. You'll never be lonely again."

23

POLLY WALKED UP FROM THE VILLAGE on Fifth Avenue, her hands in her jacket pockets, her face tense with concentration. It was a morning for concern. Her appointment with Sol Franklin was for lunch.

"Why are you calling?" He had sounded suspicious.
"Don't you remember me?"
"Of course!"
"Can I speak with you?"
"You're speaking to me."
"Can I see you?"
He had paused. "Are you in trouble?"
"No."
"That's a relief."
"I want to talk."
"Talk to him. My son."
"He's hard to talk to."
"You're telling me!"
"I'll be brief. I promise you."
"A girl as pretty as you doesn't have to promise so much."

She walked slowly. She heard mothers shouting at their children at the Twenty-fifth Street Park. There, slumped behind cigarettes on the park benches, their ears attuned to the special cries of their children, able to distinguish among whines and shouts for help, they sat like leathery appendages to some husband's career, and she felt sorry for them. Marriage was no bed of roses.

She entered Sol's building. She refused to be intimidated by the enormous company and advanced purposefully toward the receptionist, her white gloved hands rigid at her sides.

The woman said "Yes?" without looking up.

"Mr. Franklin, please. My name is Polly Gang."

The woman put down her paper, sat straight in her chair, and paid attention.

"Do you have an appointment, Miss Gang?"

"I do. For twelve-fifteen."

"I see." The receptionist appraised the Chanel suit and dialed her telephone. She announced Polly to someone inside. She pointed toward a red door.

"Go in there, sweetie, and walk as far as you can. Mr. Franklin's secretary will meet you and take you the rest of the way."

Polly finally was ushered into Sol's office after a series of doors, corridors, and two secretaries, both of whom seemed to memorize her outfit as they introduced themselves.

When she knocked, Sol opened his office door himself. He smiled nervously and pointed to a Danish modern chair near his Danish modern desk.

"Nice to see you."

She held out her gloved hand and he shook it in a weak grip. He sat behind his desk.

She folded her arms and smiled. "You promised me lunch."

He nodded. "I got us a table at Doliner's. It's nearby. The food isn't so hot, but it's noisy."

He watched her warily. "Shoot. What's on your mind? We'll leave for the restaurant as soon as they bring in some letters for me to sign. I know all about you. I believe in putting my cards on the table."

"I do too." She moved her chair closer to his desk. "There's the question of Helga."

He reddened. "Certain things you don't discuss with girls. Bodily functions and sex."

"The fact of her pregnancy is why I'm here. Suppose she is pregnant? It alters things."

"It sure does! If that girl is carrying his son, I want to know about it. There's more here than just him. It makes me a grandfather."

"You'd like that?"

"Not necessarily," he said gruffly. "I wouldn't mind it if he loved her. I don't approve of promiscuity."

He stared at her fixedly.

"Aaron has spoken of you often."

Sol flicked his hand at the air. "That kid!"

He indicated his office with a sweep of his arm.

"This could be his, the whole shooting match. He wants to be a painter! Why would a boy turn down an opportunity like this just so he can show off? If you're thinking of marrying him, talk some sense into him. There's a lot of money to be made here."

"I wasn't speaking of marriage."

He said slyly, "I'll change the subject. What'll we talk about?"

"Do you want me to tell you the truth?"

He scratched his double chin. "Not necessarily."

"I don't know if he loves me."

Sol thought that was funny. He coughed on his cigar. "You're a sweet kid. A child. How old are you? Twenty-one? Twenty-one is a kid. Forget it. What's the difference? Nineteen or twenty-one." He considered her for a moment. "Listen. Do you love him?"

She nodded.

"If you love him, let him find himself. That's my advice."

"You mean I should forget him?"

"Don't get dramatic. I simply suggested that you give him time. A kid like that, why he's liable to do any crazy thing." He uncrossed his legs. "How about that lunch?" He pulled back her chair as she rose. He offered her his arm and said cheerfully, "By God, you smell good!"

24

AARON SPOKE TO DR. BREST: "I considered my adolescence a time of hallucination and acne. Furious erections came and went like Judas goats that led me, exposed, to gymnasium dances. Despite the Lifebuoy soap and Sen Sen and concave postures, the hard-on announced me like a Papal bulletin."

The doctor said: "I can't discuss this on my doorstep."

Aaron gazed down at the round bald head.

"I'm going back to school tomorrow."

Brest spoke. "What is that painting you shove in my face?"

"I did it," he said expansively, holding it up. "What do you think?"

"I'm an analyst, not an art critic." He paused. "Tell me. I am curious. Why is it you do not call for appointments like everybody else?"

"I don't need an hour. Just a minute or so."

"My fee is seventy-five dollars a session. This is not a discount house."

The door opened, exposing Flood, his coat wrapped protectively about his thin body. He pointed accusingly.

"That's the boy, Dr. Brest. He's the one who broke the other boy's nose. Watch him at all times."

"Moment, Mr. Flood."

The door slammed shut.

Aaron said, "Before you go, I want to say this. Helga is keeping the baby."

Brest began to laugh. His fat stomach shook beneath his vest and jacket.

"Ya? Do you marry her?"

"What's so funny?"

"Answer, please. Do you?"

"No."

"But you said . . ."

"She's keeping it all the same. She's going to raise it at home. It's a gift for her mother."

"A very funny story."

Aaron nodded and held the painting towards the doctor, who squinted. He grinned. "You are serious? She actually keeps the baby? It's fantastic! What a gesture!"

"What do you think?"

"About what?"

"This picture."

"What about this picture?"

"Should I sell it or keep it?"

Brest answered impatiently. "You must stop this nonsense. I am not an art dealer. You remind me of a patient I had once in Vienna. A hit-and-run driver. You know what this is?"

"I'm no such thing!"

"You are just like him. Only unconsciously. You bang into people and rush away from the scene of the accident. Archie Fellows tells me things. Flood informs on you. What you do, you dash about like a man in a speeding automobile. You inadvertently hit someone. In the case of Helga Fern, you impregnate. You also do this to me. You bang into my door. You exchange some words. You then leave the scene of the crime."

"That is not completely true."

"Of course not. Nothing is. I merely say, you remind me of this person in Vienna."

"What happened to him?"

"He ended in jail. I am not suggesting you should be in jail."

He held out his hand and shook Aaron's firmly.

"Goodbye. I see you again. When you finish your school. Maybe we patch you together, Archie and I, so you make some good paintings."

"No one can sum me up. I'm no synopsis. I'm a whole person. People put asterisks on my ears, then explain me in footnotes."

25

"SHE'S OUT," Gus informed him. "I've given you fair warning!"

Polly appeared wearing a black velvet dress. She passed her father, kissed him on the cheek, and took Aaron's hand. They stood together on the brownstone step.

"I'm going out, Daddy. With Aaron. You might as well get used to it."

Gus buttoned his wrinkled jacket and adjusted his bow tie.

"Do you disobey your father?"

"Oh, Daddy," she sighed.

"Forget him." Aaron started his car.

"I don't know what to do. He's getting worse. Ever since she died."

"You have your own life!"

"I'll never forgive myself."

He stopped the car. "I want to ask you something. Why were you at college when she was dying?"

She stared dumbly ahead. "I wanted Daddy with me.

Without her. She got sick and went to the hospital, and I had him alone. I cooked for him and cleaned and sent his clothes to the tailor. I showed him how nice I could make things. How perfect it could be with just the two of us. I pleaded, I insisted he take me to college. I was awful."

He drove nervously in the evening traffic, piloting the large Buick as if it were a sports car, dodging in and out, avoiding the slow lanes, weaving and feinting and getting onto the Long Island Expressway with such speed that she touched his arm and pleaded for caution.

"You're much too fast. You'll hit somebody."

He reduced speed. "You're right," he said judiciously. He remained in the right-hand lane and observed the traffic laws.

"Where are we going?"

"To my studio."

She mused, "What does any of it mean?"

He stared directly ahead and said seriously: "I am your Maginot Line."

"Oh," she said bleakly, "I wish it were true."

He spoke forcefully. "I have never lied to you. When I saw you, I saw quality!"

She sat docilely, her hands folded on her lap.

"Where are you taking me?"

"You know where. My studio."

"We'll go to bed together if we're left alone."

He spoke with relief: "I know it."

"I don't think we should. I feel awful. I want to. I swear I do. But not tonight. I feel so wretched, I couldn't bear it. I've done a raw thing."

"Let me say this: Concerning yourself with mothers is a waste of time. How do you know she wanted him there? Maybe she wanted to die in private."

"Maybe you're right!"

He had never met her mother, so he didn't know. He tightened his grip on the steering wheel. He realized he had never really met his own mother. She was a blank screen.

When they came upon his studio, he parked the car and led her in. Entering, he switched on the lights and asked if she was hungry. When she said no, he took her hand and they mounted the short flight of stairs that led to the skylight studio. They sat in wooden chairs near his easel.

"Wait," he said. He ran back to the car.

She wandered about the room. A window at the far side, near the bed, overlooked Long Island Sound. Above her, she could see the pale quarter moon. Stacks of paintings leaned neatly against all four walls and the room smelled faintly of varnish and turpentine and expensive soap.

When he returned, he went immediately to the easel with a large brightly painted picture.

"Oh!" she exclaimed. "It's your father."

"It's just a man at a piano."

"It looks like your father."

"That's a coincidence. It's no one special. What do you think?"

She paused. "It's neat!"

"You don't like it, do you?" He slumped.

"I never said that."

"Well, do you?"

"Not much."

He shrugged.

"You don't mind?"

"It's a good painting. The best I've ever done."

He covered it with the paper.

"Can I see the ones against the wall?"

"Some other time. Don't you want to eat? I have an ice box downstairs."

"What should I do about my father?"

"I'm very tired of him."

"Well, what do I do?"

A squall of rain sprayed Long Island Sound, and out past the wharves tarpaulined pleasure boats bobbed in choppy surf.

Standing in semidarkness, he said: "I brought you here. I want to marry you."

"Oh, sure you do. But how about Gus? Who will Gus have?"

He studied her. Her face shone with sad self-assurance; a picture in a college yearbook. He walked forward. He placed his hands on her shoulders.

She sat on the floor, her arms clasping her knees. Somewhat surprised, she said, "I can't."

He sat beside her, avoiding her. He tried touching her thick hair. She raised her face, arching her throat, smiled wistfully, and lowered her head.

"Are you crying?"

"Maybe. I cry when I think about Gus."

Without warning, deliberately, she began undressing herself. She unzipped her dress, pulled it over her head, dropped it on the chair, shook loose her hair, and began, matter-of-factly, to unhook her brassiere. She undid her garterbelt, pushed down her stockings into two nylon puddles, and stepped out of her black panties.

Her perfection stunned him: her wide hips, her short legs. He stared with gratitude.

She turned in a slow circle, then turned half again around with her back toward him.

She looked over her shoulder. Fully dressed, he walked around the easel and joined her. He touched her carefully. He embraced her from the rear to gather her up. He felt his cheeks ache from the wide grin that opened his face. She was more beautiful than he had remembered her. How could it be possible? All that beauty crowded into one small body. He clasped her tightly. He dropped to his knees and moved his face over her.

"Take off your clothes." She pushed him away.

He did. They faced each other like two tentative nudists rather than lovers.

She examined him. His body retained the trace of a sunburn. His flat chest was hairless, as were his legs and arms.

He turned off the light. In the darkness he heard her disembodied voice say, "All right."

He pulled her to him. She opened her mouth against his. It held a vague touch of lemon or a kind of blossom he couldn't place.

"Ow!" He pushed her back. She had bitten his lip. "That hurt!"

"Pay attention!" She kissed him hard on his bruised lip, humming against it, and gently chewed it. He could taste the salty blood, and prepared to complain, when he felt her leave him. He heard her run to the light switch, turn it on, and rush to the bed. Her thick hair spanking her back, she trotted towards the bed. She sat on it, her head propped on her elbows, and regarded him carefully. He remained by the easel, tentatively touching his lip with his tongue. He watched her, enjoying the spectacle of her short body turning and falling forward and stretching out, stomach down on the bed, her bare feet jammed insolently into his snow-white pillow case.

Suddenly, almost against his will, he bounded across the room, leaping through the air in a flying tackle that terminated next to her on the bed, causing her to bounce once and topple on top of him. They wrestled, pummeling the bed, arms and legs tangled, tugging, pulling, so filled with exhilaration that they forgot, momentarily, the seriousness of purpose that had brought them together.

When he awakened with his face pillowed on her warm belly, he was surrounded by her intimate odor.

She stirred. She felt for him, dropping her arm and drawing her fingertips lightly along his neck. He slid his body upwards. Half asleep, he held her in the grasp of ownership.

"I couldn't let you go," she said. She cradled his head in the crook of her arm and pressed his face against her. "Our bodies fit."

He agreed. He closed his eyes. He dozed. He kissed her.

They slept and, as the dawn exposed them slowly, vaguely illuminating the chairs, tables, their own gray bodies, she turned on her side, wondered where she was, touched his hair, and sat straight up, wide awake and mildly troubled. She shook his shoulder and repeated, "Wake up, wake up."

He opened one eye. She was bouncing on the bed and talking to herself.

"Polly! What's wrong?"

"I can't marry you," she said desperately. "You may have your paintings, but I have a responsibility."

He rubbed his eyes. "You mean Gus?"

"I've been thinking. I could be happy with you, but I wouldn't be safe."

"Go back to sleep."

"I'd be safe with Toby."

26

SOL HAD LOTS OF MOXIE. He advanced across his enormous estate with bouncing optimistic purpose and checked his trees and lawn and privet hedge with quick eyes—quick as a sandpiper, that frenzied bird who runs about the beaches taking inventory.

He considered Aaron a lovely boy destined for failure. A good boy, nice to his mother; but a drifter. In his day (Sol's) you had to slug it out. It was no picnic living in East Boston. Not that he didn't understand his son. That was a lot of crap. What's not to understand? It was a question of money. He himself had quit school in the sixth grade and Aaron went out with Gentile girls.

He had a son who went to college, while he, Sol, was self-educated—which he admitted was not so marvelous because self-educated people, with all due respect, were always recently learning something that everyone else already knew.

He removed from his breast pocket a large cigar. It was coarse, black, and heavily veined, with a blue-black lumpy wrapper. Made of specially grown sun-ripened tobacco, it

157

cost a dollar even and projected from the middle of his red face like a hose on a hydrant.

He lit a kitchen match with his plump thumbnail, lit his cigar (the first of the day), and inundated himself with great clouds of solace. "Ah," he said.

They had lived in the Bronx at the time. He walked the streets all night giving cigars to total strangers. "I just had a son," he said. All over the Bronx, total strangers were smoking Coronas in the middle of the Depression.

Of course Alma mollycoddled him. They tried for more kids, without success. It wasn't easy. One boy. One little cocker taking up her time. Climbing in their bed, getting close to Mommy. How about him? Was he short-changed? You bet your life he was. He should have had a daughter. "Daddy's home," and a big kiss. A daughter's kiss was worth fifty handshakes from a big-shot son.

Looking back on it, he knew their bed was always filled with him. A son with bad dreams, a son with fever, lonely or frightened. He wondered why he had never cheated on her. (He wasn't that kind of hairpin.)

. . . Well, not necessarily. Rhoda Mergolin was a looker in Accounts Payable. A girl named Mary, also in the bookkeeping department (maybe in receivables to balance things) had the nerve to tell him he was *cute*. He should have fired her, except they were in the elevator going up. It embarrassed him, a girl young enough to . . . well, younger by a long shot. She made him nervous all week. He couldn't keep his mind on business. It gave him indigestion, since he *was* kind of cute. Finally, it gave him such a migraine, he took a room at the Commodore with a bottle of milk of magnesia and slept all afternoon and had a complete purge and got rid of the headache until that night on the train when he kept picturing her in unnatural positions and got off at Bayside and took a cab back to the office. He looked her name up in the personnel file and called her up and his mouth was so dry and he was so dizzy he figured himself for a coronary.

"I knew you'd call," she'd said when what seemed like hours later she answered and he told her it was her boss who was desperate and in great need of her and for Christ's sake keep your mouth shut.

A sweet kid. Very skinny with a generous nature. He explained she'd have to quit later. She agreed. She even said it was worth it, which he doubted since she had a good job and he wasn't as young as he once was. He gave her a hundred-dollar war bond and a ticket to Miami. It took him a half a year to stop feeling ashamed of himself. Not because he'd cheated, but for letting her go.

Aaron took after him. He had an eye for the girls. Sol thought of his own father, a silly man who ate herring from a barrel and read Spinoza and never earned a red cent, while his wife (a saint) ran the store and wrapped the lox and swept up and worshiped the old man.

Sol walked faster as he crossed the road and turned towards Aaron's studio. It lay down a ridge that sloped gently towards a Sol-made brook, over which a Japanese bridge, rich with vines and grape leaves, curved downwards towards the blue gravel driveway that circled the front of the house. The grass that dampened the high polish of his shoe-tops was curried and mowed by two Japs who took kickbacks from the manure dealer, the topsoil dealer, and the seed people. He believed in graft. It gave a man incentive. His two top salesmen were thieves. They padded expenses, faked invoices, and stole from petty cash. They even stole stamps. But each year they were the highest grossers.

How about Aaron? Could it be that he sired a loser? . . . Of course! There it was in a nutshell. . . . The boy had skipped a generation. . . . Or maybe he inherited it from his mother's parents. There was a proud heritage. They whined their way in steerage and traveled third-class all their lives. They never seized America. They never left the hold of that ship for thirty years. Sam and Rose, where are you now? Is Heaven like a ship?

He loved America. He clapped when they showed the flag. What the hell. . . . He was perpetually astounded by Zionists. When you're surrounded by anti-Semites, leave your yarmelka home. Be a Jew on your own time, not on America's.

Usually his son slept late. It seemed he was up. He thought he saw a figure pass by the studio window.

He walked closer, taking little fat man's steps. Tossing his cigar in a soft arc behind him, he pictured the two of them riding to town together, chatting.

He passed by Aaron's Buick parked badly in the driveway, its rear tires smearing the damp grass. Maybe he had a chippy in there. Maybe he should clear his throat. And as he deliberated, he saw in the distance, absolutely naked in the downstairs window, a beautiful young girl with a white rear end and very small breasts. Breasts like small portions of whipped cream.

She bent down to scratch her foot, exposing a surprising view of her womanhood. The girl hadn't seen him. She turned once and rubbed her behind. It looked as if she were kneading two loaves of fresh white bread.

He felt terribly warm. He wiped his face with a silk handkerchief. He turned away. "Lovely," he thought. He momentarily envied his son. Not for style or elegance, but for a few lousy years. That was his edge because Sol could, in the old days, charm a snake. Oh, he'd had beautiful women. He wasn't complaining. But God. To be thin and young. What a terrible thing to be old, when you *are* old.

Sol shook his great round head. He cursed himself for peeping and for being sixty. He made a fast about-face, but wanted to peep again, to see that flat white stomach, the gray skin with sleep upon it. He marveled at her body, this young bimbo his son had found; and he controlled the need to march into his son's studio (*his* studio, as a matter of fact) and seize her. She would laugh. An old little fat guy.

He reconsidered. Hells bells, he thought. Not so old. Once he was the fastest kid in the neighborhood. He remembered foot races on Porter Street. He outran Manny Coupleoff who raced for YMHA varsity. He could still go like a bat out of hell. Wiping his red face he had to smile to himself. An old cocker. Good luck to Aaron! Good luck with his life.

He became angry. His face grew dangerously red. What right had that punk kid to lay around the house. Spoiled. He stood still and felt his blood rush to his neck and face. His body seemed to swell with it. He felt the delicious dizziness that banged into him when, at such moments of glorious anger, his whole plump body filled with blood like a swelling zeppelin. What did he think life was?—a rest cure? No. It was too goddamn much! Lying around like a goddamned Valentine.

Inside Aaron's house, Polly patted her stomach and finished dressing. In the morning light her black cocktail dress seemed silly.

27

SOL WENT IN TO WORK. He felt tired. Like a descending balloon, he sighed and lowered his weary frame. He sat in his chair behind his desk. . . . The pep was gone.

Another autumn . . . another signal, a call to arms: Begin. He'd done so much . . . built and wrestled . . . failed, stumbled and built again. . . . Accomplish. . . . A business. . . . A wealthy man. . . . He rubbed his face with both his hands; he searched his body, probed and touched: his passive flesh, an inner tube; beneath a silk suit, useless weight.

His lassitude confused him. . . . Should he be worn at sixty?

Why not? . . .

He worked his head off . . . for thirty years. . . . While others soldiered on the job or slept late or painted pictures, he slugged like a champion.

Life had done this . . . drained him . . . bled him. Like a fortress in the sand, his walls were washed away.

Autumn scared him: a new climate . . . even a bully wears out. He owned the business . . . he owned his son . . . (nice kid).

He couldn't focus. He plucked at paper on his cluttered desk. Expense accounts. (Can't anyone eat for under twenty dollars?)

He shot his head up. He arranged himself. He touched his tie: someone was in the corridor.

"You here?" It was Aaron. In the doorway, serious, troubled.

Why should a father owe his son? . . . What about sons, don't they have debts? . . . No time for weaklings . . . make your bed . . . cry alone.

"I thought I'd find you."

"So?"

"If you haven't had lunch . . ."

Sol's face had altered, Aaron thought. It was emptied of its lively look. A face seen through a clouded glass: the vital face was cautious now, as if a cloth had wiped the color off.

Aaron pressed on, his troubles forcing him to speak. "Polly won't marry me."

Too tired for confessions, Sol said: "Polly? Was she at your house this morning?"

"Did you see her?"

"Maybe," he said quickly. "I was out taking a walk."

"She's the one."

Aaron slumped. He dropped listlessly into a leather chair.

"Everybody gets married. . . . I married your mother thirty years ago. I haven't regretted a day. I never dried a dish. I never changed a diaper. We never wanted for anything. . . . Give them servants, that's the ticket. . . ."

"Children are the reason to get married. . . . Grandchildren."

"I don't need charity."

"I didn't mean that . . ."

"Grow up," Sol said impatiently. "Get a grip on yourself."

With great exertion Sol heaved himself out of his chair and onto his feet. He braced himself on the edge of the desk. "I'm coming down with a cold," he said. "Change of seasons."

Aaron said, "You don't look well. . . . Why don't you lie down."

Sol's manner softened. He smiled. "I'll live. . . . After fifty it's all patchwork."

He moved slowly to the door of his office. "Come on, old-timer. I'll buy you lunch." He seemed stronger. He beckoned like a traffic cop. "Let's go. Stop worrying. . . . For a man like you, there are plenty of girls."

Sol had eaten in Doliner's for the first time fifteen years earlier. He tasted their sauerbraten, their potato pancakes, the loganberry pancakes, and the schnitzel, and he fell in love. He ate there six days a week. He sent the chef one hundred dollars each Christmas; he tipped the hatcheck girl a dollar a day and sat by the low window at his own private table. Once, he had tried to buy the restaurant, hoping to convert it into a private club for executives, but Hans Doliner declined his offer. During the late thirties, when it appeared that Hans would go bankrupt, Sol loaned him twenty thousand dollars to stay open, so in a sense, even though the money had been returned, he had a proprietary interest.

Aaron followed him across the sawdust floor and seated himself at the reserved table.

He had never seen the old man with his guard down. He felt a surge of warmth so unexpected, so dredged from some foreign part of his nervous system, that he blinked.

His father was speaking. He jabbed the air with his thumb as if the space before him contained important buttons. "People complain their whole lives," his father said. He spoke wonderingly, his voice slow and dreamlike. "About their jobs, their children, their automobile. Wives complain about husbands and vice versa. . . . 'Hang up your clothes

... shovel the walk ... empty the garbage ... change the kid ...' Know what they're really saying? I'll tell you: They're really saying, 'Why don't you love me?'" He slapped the air with his plump hand. "Aaaa," he snorted, gaining momentum. "When all is said and done, what does it mean? You kill yourself to make a buck and it's never enough!

"I don't mean your mother.... She's a saint. She never once asked for anything. Whatever she got, it was enough. I'm talking about most of the miserable bastards who whine through life like civil servants, who settle for anything and demand everything. All over the world, at five in the morning you can hear them. All whining, 'What's in it for me? How come I got gypped and short-changed?' ... They short-changed themselves, the bastards!"

He examined the menu. "I'll have the liverwurst plate," he said conversationally. "And a stein of dark beer."

Aaron chewed his lip. "Is this an attack?" he asked sharply. "Do you mean me?"

Sol smiled. "Ah, not you, Aaron." He jabbed his son's sleeve experimentally. "You're a sweet boy, Aaron. You got no drive, that's your trouble. You haven't found yourself."

He snapped his fingers at the hovering waiter. "I'll have the liverwurst. Give my son whatever he wants." He turned to Aaron. "You want a steak, or lobster?"

"Make it liverwurst," Aaron said. He had no appetite.

"I've had my turn," Sol said philosophically. "The old order dies.... It's like wheat. It grows. You cut it down. A new crop comes." He clapped his hands smartly. The waiter, halfway to the kitchen, turned quickly. "Two dark beers," Sol said. "In steins."

Sol jackknifed forward: a fierce contraction toppled him onto the restaurant table. Shaken by a spasm, his body shook and stiffened. It jerked to the side like a hooked marlin. He thrashed and shot straight up, his face parted in anger. A wild cry of torment: "My arm . . . my arm!" His left arm flopped pathetically. His face fell downward, hit like a gavel, and slid sickeningly into his platter of food. His Irish tenor's voice escaped: "I think I'm blind."

He realized where he was: a public place. "It will pass. . . ." He gripped the table edge with his right hand. "Indigestion. . . . I can't seem to see."

Someone from the corner said: "I think he's drunk."

A waitress came. The manager too. "Get a doctor. It's Mr. Franklin."

Aaron watched the horrifying spectacle. "Don't die. . . . What can I do? . . ." He jumped about, out of control. "Ambulance," he shouted pushing back the circling group.

Sol lay very still, his great red face deathly quiet. Aaron wiped a bit of liverwurst from his father's forehead.

"What happened?" The manager touched his sleeve. Aaron pulled his arm away. He stared, transfixed, too stunned to answer. He mumbled to himself . . . "My father. He's dead."

He placed his arms around the crumpled body and hugged it.

With the help of two waiters he lowered Sol to the floor. There on the carpet by their table, his son's lap for a pillow, Sol lay stiff and untroubled, his bright blue eyes staring upwards through his polished bifocals, his mouth half open as if to cheer.

Aaron spoke to him: "Hang on, Pop," he said numbly. And as he spoke he knew: his father was dead already. Life had shot out of him like a torpedo out of its tube.

Aaron heard the siren. He glanced at the door. A white whale of an ambulance waited by the curb. Interns jumped out. They rushed at him, their black bags brushing their knees like sample cases. On they came like traveling salesmen.

They put Sol on a stretcher and closed his eyes. They snatched him into the air and proceeded towards the door, in step, like the front and rear of a vaudeville horse.

Aaron climbed into the ambulance behind them. He sat on a bench next to his father and thought about him. How embarrassed his father would have been.

Tears splashed his sweater and fell on his limp hands. He mumbled: "I've lost him." He was gone. He thought: I'll miss him.

His father shifted on the stretcher as the ambulance turned a corner. He bounced like luggage, then flopped back. For a moment Aaron started. He was alive! He looked again. No. Dead as before. A terrible anger shook him. What right had he to die? Who would look after Alma? And the business? The ambulance jolted Sol. "Lie still," Aaron shouted. He held Sol's gray fedora and topcoat on his lap. (Someone—the manager maybe—had placed it there.) He pressed the cloth to his cheek. He gazed down at the bland face. Death had stolen the prideful look and erased a museum of expressions.

28

SOL WOULD HAVE LIKED THE TURNOUT. Well-dressed people overcrowded the second floor of the East Side funeral home and lined the stairway with such congestion that a loudspeaker was installed to broadcast the eulogy to those who couldn't be seated.

Behind the casket, a mountain of flowers. Sol seemed light as a doll, stretched out and powdered. They had rouged his cheeks and parted his hair and retouched the ravaged face he brought to his death. It wasn't his father. They had thrown his father away and substituted a ventriloquist's dummy. . . .

A Reformed rabbi spoke Hebrew. Aaron sat dry-eyed, marveling at the display.

Breaking through the treacly speech came the shrill cry of Aaron's mother. She pounded her feet.

Aaron had never heard such weeping: full-grown men, men who looked like elder statesmen, crying over Sol. He stared from face to face: the Supreme Court of America seemed to mourn his father, elegant, florid, white-haired gents, men of the old school. "You don't know me, son, but

I knew your dad. Dreadful thing, his passing on . . . a generous soul . . . a great American."

Who were they, these polished Gentiles? Others too: in from Great Neck, suit and cloakers, gentle people in Vicuna topcoats: "A lovely man, your father. . . . A generous person." The salesmen, the cutters, the accounting department.

All Sol's sisters, in from Hempstead. All the old gang, Herzog, Cohen.

The man who sold him papers waited in a shabby coat and shook his hand. "Your father was decent."

Homer Bienheim, the banker, the man responsible for the Company's line of credit, hugged Aaron more for support than sympathy. He seemed near collapse. "I loved him, Aaron. . . . He was a tough bastard, but you had to love him."

Aaron said: "He had great energy, Homer."

Aaron helped his mother stand. He grasped her arm and guided her towards the line of rented limousines that waited. She lurched against him, her face, veiled as a beekeeper's, sobbing and shaking.

"He's gone," she cried. "I've lost him."

Aaron placed his arms about her. "Oh, oh, oh," she said.

He wanted to comfort her. She had him. She had her friends and the Company.

"I'm here, Mom," he said.

She pulled her arm away and straightened her back. She snorted. "HE'S NOT HERE ANYMORE!" She banged her hands together and cried loudly.

"What can I do?" he asked, trying to calm her.

"You?" She raised her black veil. Her eyes were swollen from crying. She faced him. She caught her breath. She pointed a finger, not at him but at the sky above them. "He was a MAN!"

"I know," he said.

She placed the veil over her face and answered him quietly. "We will all miss him." She briskly seated herself in the first limousine, directly behind the hearse. "Ride with me, Aaron."

29

THE PLACE WHERE SOL WAS CREMATED was a gray, prison-like structure in Jersey, a few miles out of New York. There Alma stood alone, supporting herself on a brass railing as her husband's coffin slid into a furnace, flared once in a gasp of fire, like the finale of a fireworks display, and disappeared. She was strangely quiet. Aaron saw her hands grip the rail and feared she might topple and join her husband, but she raised her head and backed away. Dry-eyed she searched for him, joined him, and taking his arm, led the procession of friends and relatives out of the damp building where they reentered the black limousines and returned to Long Island.

Later that evening when they were alone they sat together at the dining room table. Her controlled manner, her matter-of-factness, so surprised him that he attempted clumsily to reassure her. "He had a good life."

Alma Franklin narrowed her gray eyes. When she spoke, her voice, which had repeated itself like a Greek chorus while her husband lived, took on a new firm, businesslike tone that caused him to examine her suspiciously. "Don't worry about it."

She smoothed her skirt and placed a cigarette in her mouth, a thing she had never done. After lighting it, she tossed the pack of Luckies on the table and inhaled deeply.

"He was opposed to my smoking. He was an old-fashioned man, your father. In many ways." She squinted as smoke rushed from her nostrils in twin streams. "I sneaked them when he wasn't home. I'm not ashamed of that fact. He had enough to worry him without a wife who smoked."

"You'll miss him," he said in an expression of hope rather than explanation.

"Don't!" she warned, in her strange voice. "I don't need help in mourning. He was my life, not yours. You gave him a few pleasures. I was his right arm."

What impressed him most was her size. She rose from her chair, her chin out, her head tilted, and continued growing at an extraordinary rate, like a trick done with mirrors. Perhaps his own grief caused this deception. But this much he knew: his own mother, who took up no more space than a familiar piece of furniture, had become a formidable presence at the far end of the table.

"Who will look after you?" he asked, hoping the sound of her actual speaking voice would so startle her, it would reduce her to manageable proportions.

She put out her cigarette in her coffee cup.

"So much for manners," she said, speaking in her new voice. "You ask who? I say, 'No one!'"

"I'll stay with you for a bit, then I'll go back to school."

She shrugged. "Suit yourself. The house is yours to come and go."

"But, Mother," he insisted, hoping to share his loss, "won't you miss him?"

She considered his question. She folded her hands before her as a child would in school and explained her position with such finality and precision that his mouth dropped open.

"Life is for the living. While he lived, no man received better service. I loved that man. I would have killed for him. A wife's love is so sacred, nobody can understand its depth. While you gallivanted around making girls pregnant and studying art and visiting psychoanalysts I cherished that man. I held him to my body when he returned from work so weary it was a crime. I bathed him. That shocks you, but I did that and more. Enemas too! I denied him nothing. I created a life for that man. What was he? He was a genius. A wild cossack. And I made him a home. An oasis. A cool, shady place to rest his head. I gave my life away when he married me. I was the dowry he got. Every nerve and muscle. A slave, a wife, a mistress, a dog! Now, it's over. Everything. The service ends. Even wives get time off. I have served without complaint, without nagging, without a cry of pain. Served, waited, and loved him so dearly, he never knew how much. Men never do. They take for granted. Like you are now. You take me for granted. What am I, a hotel? You say you'll stay. Why? Are you worried? A new phase begins now. I am no longer Sol's right arm. I am me. Alma Franklin. A widow. A mother. But also a person. You are a transient passing through. A good boy, an artist maybe. My advice to you is go to Paris and be a painter. Write me a letter. But don't molest my spirit. I have earned this vacation and I promise you—I'm taking it."

30

GUS SAT IN HIS BATHROBE and regarded his daughter over a tumbler of rye. She paced the living room.

"It's not like him, not calling. One thing about him: he always calls."

She had been to Sol's funeral. Uninvited, she waited in the doorway, behind the rows of seated mourners. Aaron had appeared, drawn and corpselike; his black suit worried her. She had never seen him in a necktie.

The New York Times had devoted two columns on the obituary page, and a blurred two-inch photograph of a grinning fat man under the headline: "Business Community Honors Solomon Franklin." They wrote of Sol's Silver Star, of his many charities. His son was described as an artist, his wife as a leader in Jewish philanthropies.

The doorbell rang. Toby carried a large basket of fruit, covered with cellophane.

"Hi, Polly," he said. His sunburned face beamed down at her. "Helga told me young Franklin is off to Europe."

She nodded brusquely. "Come in."

He held out the basket.

"I thought we'd see him off. All's well that ends well. I want to see him on that ship actually as it sails away. I don't wish him harm. (After all, he lost his father.) But I'm glad he's going. It couldn't be far enough!"

He strode up to Gus and shook his hand.

"How are you, sir? You're looking fit."

Gus quickly withdrew his hand. "I'll make a deal with you. No more handshakes. Acknowledge me less physically." He massaged his fingers.

Polly said, "Put down the basket."

Toby opened the cellophane and extracted an apple. "Fruit, sir?"

Gus grunted. Polly paced. Toby bit sharply into the apple. He chewed vigorously.

"I need your help, Toby. It's a lot to ask."

He answered proudly, "Anything I can do for you, I'll do."

"Be patient with me. I've got to see Aaron."

Swallowing, he nodded sadly. "Mother warned me."

She frowned. "I want to say goodbye to Aaron." Her eyes filled. "You're both trying to stop me. You and Daddy."

Gus sipped his drink and mildly protested: "I've done no such thing. I'm as permissive a parent as you could hope for."

Toby said, "Don't cry."

She pounded her fist in her open palm. "I'm trying to explain. It's difficult."

Toby said, "Your father and I will wait for you. Don't be upset." He turned to Gus. "Don't you agree, sir?"

Gus shrugged and examined the ice cubes in his glass. Polly dried her eyes with a tissue.

"I have to hurry. The boat leaves in an hour."

She arrived, by taxi, twenty minutes later at the 57th Street Pier, overtipped the driver, and ran up the steps towards the visitors gate, where she was informed by a guard that visitors were forbidden to enter. "The All-Ashore has been announced."

She regarded him sternly and pointed her gloved hand. "It isn't fair."

"Sorry, miss. No exceptions."

She measured the green picket fence separating her from the pier. She stood on tiptoes in an effort to see Aaron, but passengers blocked her view.

"I must get on that pier. It's really important."

"It's too late for that," the guard said, comfortable in the rules.

"I never planned," she replied. "I acted on impulse."

He folded his arms. "The first All-Ashore has sounded."

She scanned the fence, seeking an opening. Near the elevator behind her, a porter loaded steamer trunks on dollies.

"I need your help," she said. "I must get through the gate."

He paused.

She kept her back to the guard and whispered, "How much tip do you get for one trunk?"

"Depends. Around a dollar." He prepared to move past her, when she hurriedly reached into her purse and extracted a twenty-dollar bill.

"What are you doing?"

"I'm offering you money to get me on the pier. It's quite easy. Stack a few trunks. One on top of the other. Leave room for me in the middle as if it were a house of building blocks. Think you can manage?"

"I'll get caught. He'll see you and then I'm in trouble. I got work to do."

She sighed. "Twenty-five dollars. I only have twenty-five dollars. We'll go behind a pillar and fix up the tiny house.

Drape the front and back with a blanket or golf bags or something."

He shook his head. "It's against the law. It's smuggling."

"No, it isn't. We're in America, for Pete's sake. I'm meeting a friend, you see. It's important. He's waiting for me on the pier. He's rich. He would be ever so grateful to you for bringing me to him. There's no telling what he'd be willing to do."

He studied her. "He's waiting, this friend?"

She nodded vigorously. "I knew you'd agree."

"It'll cost you fifty dollars. If I'm going to get laid off, I got to protect my family. You sure he's got fifty dollars?"

She pulled at his arm. "Hurry! We haven't much time."

31

AARON HESITATED on the center of the gangplank. Undecided, his pictures under his arms, he heard the second "All-Ashore." When his name was called, he looked behind him and noticed a particularly overloaded dollie being pushed slowly down the pier. It teetered clumsily, righted itself, and continued, its porter struggling to keep it upright. Something about it separated it from the other luggage, causing him to watch its progress as it creaked and strained on the cement floor. What had seemed at first to be a piece of white cloth sticking out from the middle, appeared to be a white-gloved hand waving wanly from the exact center of the stack of luggage.

The glove continued to wave. As the dollie came abreast of him, he contemplated the hand. It was attached to an arm that moved it from deep inside the luggage. The hand seemed to be waving in his direction. Then he heard her voice.

"Aaron. It's me, Polly. I've come to stop you."

The white glove protruded from the middle of trunks.

It beckoned to him. It fluttered at him.

He heard a short cry behind him and turned in time to see her advancing rapidly, her white gloved hands reaching for him, her face pale, her hair disheveled. "Oh Aaron," she called, "my poor dearest."

He rushed towards her without thinking, skinning his knee on a box, meeting her in a desperate embrace. "I've been an absolute idiot." She cleared her throat and hanging on to him said, "I never knew how much I missed you. You're precious to me. You didn't call when your father died. I telephoned your mother. She said you were on your way to Paris. Why didn't you let me know?"

"I wanted to. I thought about it."

"Aaron, you should have called."

"You had Gus."

She released him and stepped back. Her eyes closed. "I can't leave Daddy. That's all there is to it. I get a sick feeling when I think of leaving."

"It's no crime to leave your parents. You might as well. If you wait, they leave you. Like my father. They cremated him. Into the oven. They had him all gussied up. They burned his Sulka tie. He just had his teeth capped."

"I've loved you all along." She sat down on a box and covered her face with her hands. "Don't leave me. Stay in New York. Don't just rush off to Europe, for Pete's sake."

"It's too late." He held out his wallet. "I have a passport. I have a ticket."

"What about your mother?"

He said grimly, "What about me?"

"Well," she began, "I'm not quite sure."

"I am orphaned," he explained. He blew his nose.

She had abused him. He had trusted her and she had abandoned him. Gus would take her as death had taken Sol.

He surveyed the noisy travelers and sensed the depression that had plagued him throughout the week. It came upon him in strange places at indeterminate moments. For no reason, tears would form. He might see an empty cab in an aimless search for customers and find his eyes damp; a movie marquee between pictures, suspended between past and future attractions, caused him to cover his face. Things that normally escaped his notice now held it: used candy wrappers, overweight children. He hoped it would stop soon, and his life would return to him. His father had been dead a week.

He had failed—not once, but every day of his waking life. Never once had he held that large head in his arms and kissed it. Not for love. Not for sentiment. For life. Hold the living, kiss while there's time.

He gazed mournfully at the ship lying white and remote at the side of the wharf; he glanced back at Polly's hand, and decided to go it alone. In Europe. The past was over, the future unreal. He needed no appendages. "Not needed on the voyage," he thought as reluctantly he presented his ticket to the uniformed people and boarded the boat.

Polly called after him, but he forced his way past shouting festive passengers dancing to the ship's band. The paintings under both his arms slowed his progress; an occasional reveler spun him around by catching a picture in passing.

He found his cabin, a small room in first class with a porthole. (Sol had told him: "If you can't go first class, stay home.")

The bed was occupied. He was ready to excuse himself when something familiar about the woman lying with her back to him caused him to look again.

"I believe there's been an error," he began.

Helga turned slowly; her large legs moved first, followed

by her wide body; finally, with a grunt, her shoulders and head faced him.

"Hi," she said. Her utter hopelessness held him immobilized.

The gloom and dejection overwhelmed him and undermined his resolve. It hampered, then it modified him.

"It's you, Helga. Like before. Behind every door, around every corner!"

He dropped his pictures and stared at her girth with fatigue. A weariness displaced his anger. A laziness spread through his body. Something about her drew him to her. Transfixed and stunned, he found himself moving towards the bed like a somnambulist, pulled inexplicably towards her white, wide arms. He approached the bed, avoiding her tiny colorless eyes. Too ashamed to recognize her, he gazed stupidly at the leaden porthole and continued his slow, measured steps towards her until he was so close, he smelled her lavender perfume and felt her coarse hair against his face. Her indolent hands lay piled in her lap. Her colorless skin waited before him. Her thin lips spoke without moving, like a ventriloquist.

"Captains can marry people."

ABOUT THE AUTHOR:

Fred Segal was born in New York and educated at the George School and Bard College. He owns an advertising agency and is also a painter whose pictures have been exhibited in New York and form part of certain New York collections. Mr. Segal's novel will be made into a motion picture and released in the winter of 1968. The author is married, the father of four children, and lives in Manhattan.